Fundraising Online

The home page of the Alzheimer's Association at: http://www.alz.org. Reprinted with permission from the Alzheimer's Association.

Fundraising Online

Using the Internet to Raise Serious Money for Your Nonprofit Organization

Gary M. Grobman
and
Gary B. Grant

White Hat Communications
Harrisburg, Pennsylvania

12-06
30%

This publication is intended to provide general information and should not be construed as legal advice or legal opinions concerning any specific facts or circumstances. Consult an experienced attorney if advice is required concerning any specific situation or legal matter. Please note that the Internet and the technology that relates to it are changing rapidly. The information in this book, while accurate to the best we can determine, will change during the life of this publication. We regret any inconvenience this may cause.

Some of the material that appears in this book originally appeared in the book *The Nonprofit Organization's Guide to E-Commerce,* and has been updated. Additional material in this book first appeared in *Contributions Magazine* in columns written by Gary M. Grobman.

Printed in the United States of America.
Editing: Linda Grobman, John Hope

Library of Congress Cataloging-in-Publication Data

Grobman, Gary M.
  Fundraising online : using the internet to raise serious money for your nonprofit organization / Gary M. Grobman and Gary B. Grant.
       p. cm.
  Includes bibliographical references and index.
  ISBN 1-929109-18-0 (alk. paper)
  1. Electronic fund raising. 2. Nonprofit organizations--Finance. I. Grant, Gary B. II. Title.
  HG177.G77 2006
  658.15'22402854678--dc22
                        2006008968

Table of Contents

Acknowledgments

John Hope and Linda Grobman were the principal editors of this book. They deserve kudos for their vision in making this book the best it could be. We would be remiss if we did not also mention Vince Hyman of Fieldstone Alliance, formerly the Wilder Publishing Center, who published our second collaborative book, *The Wilder Nonprofit Field Guide to Fundraising on the Internet.* Vince made many suggestions about the structure and appearance of *Fundraising Online,* and we are both grateful for his hard work and insights. Some of the material in this book first appeared in *Contributions Magazine* in columns by Gary Grobman. The editor of that magazine, Jerry Cianciolo, provided much inspiration and additional editing to some of the material that appears here. We wish to thank the many Webmasters, application service provider staff, development officers, nonprofit organization executive staff, and others who contributed to this book in one way or another, either through giving us permission to reprint screenshots, answering our questions, or referring us to sources both online and offline to help us find the material we needed to share with you. A special "thank you" goes out to Robert Beatty and Bookie Daniels of the Alzheimer's Association for helping us think about direct marketing side and prospect research, respectively. And finally, both of us are grateful to our families—Gary Grobman to his wife Linda and son Adam; and Gary Grant to his wife Kerry and daughters Alyann, Natalie, and Holly.

The Nonprofit FAQ at: http://www.idealist.org/ (Click on "The Nonprofit FAQ" from the menu on the left of the page). Reprinted with permission from Idealist.org/Action Without Borders.

Introduction

On December 26, 2004, a massive undersea earthquake struck in the Indian Ocean. Initial reports were that several thousand people were killed by the tsunami waves that swept through coastal communities in South Asia and Africa. It took several days before the global community recognized that these reports failed to measure the cataclysmic devastation in Indonesia, Sri Lanka, and nearly a dozen other countries. The loss of life was eventually counted in the hundreds of thousands, and entire communities were swept out to sea without a trace.

To many Americans, these communities were simply places on a map on the other side of the world. Yet something in this tragedy touched a chord with millions of Americans, and they responded by making hundreds of millions of dollars in donations to help. And to an astounding degree, much of this occurred via the Internet.

Of the $173 million raised by the International Red Cross within the first few weeks after the disaster, $73 million was donated via the organization's Web site, exceeding the total donated online after the September 11th terrorist attack. More than 45% of Catholic Relief Service's donations in response to the tragedy came online, almost $12 million. International relief organizations such as CARE, Save the Children, and Direct Relief International were all swamped with online donations.

Doctors Without Borders/Médecins Sans Frontières (MSF), recipient of the 1999 Nobel Peace Prize, took what is believed to be an unprecedented step in January 2005 and raised almost $20 million for its tsunami relief efforts—and then decided that further fundraising would be counterproductive. According to a posting on the organization's Web site within about ten days after the disaster, the organization was inundated by donations, much of it via its Web site's secure form. MSF noted that "at this time, MSF estimates that we have received sufficient funds for our currently foreseen emergency response in South Asia." MSF directed donors to donate either to the organization's general fund or to other international relief organizations.

In August 2005, hurricanes Katrina and Rita in the gulf coast of the U.S. resulted in 24-hour coverage by the news networks, followed by an almost constant appeal during commercial breaks to make cash contributions. As we write this, an amount in excess of a billion dollars appears to have been contributed online to the American Red Cross, with more coming in each day. In the first two weeks after Katrina, the Red Cross raised $439.5 million for relief efforts, and $227 million of that came in through the Internet—according to the September 15, 2005 article about it in the *Chronicle of Philanthropy.* Impressive!

The spike in online giving during 2004 and 2005 was documented in a survey conducted by the Pew Internet & American Life Project. According to this study, conducted in September and October of 2005, 26 million people had made at least one donation online, with nearly half of them contributing to Katrina relief. This translates to about 18% of Internet users, a growth from the 10% estimated to have done so in a comparable survey conducted in October 2001, just after the terrorist attacks.

When we co-wrote the book *The Wilder Nonprofit Field Guide to Fundraising on the Internet* in 1999, our enthusiastic endorsement of using the Internet for fundraising was met with some healthy skepticism from the nonprofit community. There were lingering questions about security of data, privacy, and the cost—in both time and money—of buying and maintaining the hardware and software necessary to take advantage of this new medium for attracting donations. There were also cultural barriers to overcome—such as the level of comfort donors would have to share their credit card information online and the virulent reaction most of us have to unsolicited e-mail solicitations, often considered to be "spam." Adding to the confusion was a lack of clarity with respect to how state regulators viewed charitable contributions solicited via the Internet.

Additionally, there were trust factors with which to grapple, such as whether to authorize third-party, for-profit providers to manage technology issues for nonprofit organizations. Doing so would permit leadership and staff of nonprofit organizations to focus on their primary missions. But it would also entail trusting outside organizations, which may or may not share the nonprofit's values, with both charitable contributions and sensitive data. A damaging scandal in 2003 involving PipeVine, one such third party provider—ironically a nonprofit itself— profoundly affected how we view relationships between charities and outside vendors with respect to being the steward for charitable donations. PipeVine, a donation processing application service provider, was forced to shut down operations in 2003 after it failed to deliver an estimated $19.1 million in contributions it collected, most of which were on behalf of California's Bay Area United Way. It could be years before nonprofit organizations recover from the fallout of the PipeVine scandal and again become comfortable working with outside organizations in managing online fundraising efforts.

Now, as we survey the landscape and chronicle the successes and failures of online fundraising, we have to report that many of these same issues—security, privacy, cultural adjustment, trust, and government regulation—have yet to be completely resolved to our satisfaction.

We continue to urge caution regarding these issues, but our earlier strong endorsement of using the Internet for fundraising has proven warranted as it has clearly become a vital part of the operations of virtually every nonprofit organization. We saw a glimpse of the power of online fundraising after the September 11th terrorist attacks, and more of this was unveiled during the series of devastating hurricanes that hit the southeastern United States during the 2005 storm season. Today, the online donations generated by the December 2004 tsunami and Hurricane Katrina have validated that the Internet is quickly becoming the method of choice for donors who want to respond immediately to do something tangible to help those in need, whether they live next door or on the other side of the globe.

The actual experiences of charities that look to the Internet for donations continue to be mostly positive. "Online Donations Surge" is the title of a June 10, 2004, cover story in *The Chronicle of Philanthropy* about its annual survey of online giving. That year's survey documented a 48% increase over the previous year in online gifts overall for the 157 charities that responded. Although the spike in post-September 11th online giving experienced by the American Red Cross was not sustainable in the following fiscal year, two large charities—Heifer International and the United Way of Metropolitan Atlanta—reported raising more than 15% of their total revenue online.

According to Kintera, a full-service fundraising application service provider founded in 2001, about 1% of 2004 charitable fundraising was generated by the Internet, but this percentage is increasing geometrically, thanks to the successes of the post-tsunami and Katrina appeals. A Network for Good study published in 2004 before the tsunami hit found that online giving grew by 50% compared to the previous year, to a total of $2 billion.

"The Internet has gone from being one of several channels used by nonprofits for fundraising to being – in some cases – the primary vehicle being used to generate donations," says Dr. Harry Gruber, founder and CEO of Kintera. "Key reasons for this explosion in Internet fundraising are efficiency for the organization and convenience for supporters. Donors are realizing that it's much easier to make a difference immediately with an online gift than by mailing a check."

Internet fundraising has become much more than simply having a "donate here" button linked to a page that can process credit card transactions. Online donations to charities made through third-party online charity portals, such as Network for Good and JustGive.org, have skyrocketed; both recorded a doubling of the number of people making gifts in this manner between 2002 and 2003. Network for Good boasted in a December 17, 2005, press release that it had distributed $76 million from more than 300,000 donors to 20,000 charities in the previous four years. Within days of the tsunami disaster, the charity portal recorded at least $10 million in online donations made to tsunami relief organizations. Over $1 million was donated by credit card on a single day, December 29. Donations for Katrina relief exceeded this record several-fold in August 2005.

A description of the success of the Web site Moveon (Moveon.org), in the April 17, 2003, issue of the *Chronicle of Philanthropy* provides a snapshot of the future of nonprofit advocacy and fundraising. In March 2003, this online advocacy group founded in 1998 sent a short e-mail to its two million-member e-mail list requesting donations to Oxfam America. More than 8,400 responded with online donations totaling more than $640 thousand dollars in six days. A previous appeal to raise $27,000 for an anti-war advertisement in the *New York Times* generated nearly $400,000.

Politicians from all political persuasions are scrambling to emulate the blitzkrieg fundraising success of Howard Dean's campaign for the 2004 Democratic presidential nomination. Although he ultimately didn't win his party's nomination, Governor Dean attracted thousands of supporters, mostly found through his staff's imaginative online grassroots campaign. According to news reports, this campaign started small. In the early spring of 2003, 432 supporters each pledged to find one more person to support and contribute to the Dean campaign. Within nine months, the campaign was communicating with 650,000 contributors by e-mail, with more than $50 million being raised and an average contribution of just $77. The campaign's success in mobilizing grassroots fundraising raised the bar for all political campaigns. The eventual Democratic nominee, John Kerry, reported raising $56 million on the Internet of the slightly more than $180 million the campaign raised prior to July 2004.

The direct appeal by charities to give money is only one strategy available via the Internet. New models, assisted by sophisticated advances in software technology, are providing innovative ways for charities to generate donor dollars.

According to The Hunger Site *(http://www.thehungersite.com)*, visitor clicks on a button embedded on the site's Web page resulted in 45 million cups of food being donated in 2004 for distribution to groups such as Mercy Corps and America's Second Harvest. A "blogathon" in which participants stayed up all night posting Web logs (a.k.a. "blogs") raised $20,000 for charity when the first was organized by Cat Conner in 2001, and subsequent annual blogs are doubling the amount raised each year and are becoming a world-wide phenomenon. Charity malls such as iGive *(http://www.igive.com)* provide shoppers with an incentive to shop 'til they drop; they provide a percentage of purchases to charities designated by the purchaser. According to the iGive site, $2 million has been donated to charities since the site launched in 1997 as a result of purchases made at its more than 600 participating online stores.

Much has changed in the methods used by charities to use the Internet to raise funds in the six years since we first collaborated on a book about Internet fundraising. One conclusion we have drawn from watching this online communications revolution is that online fundraising is not likely to replace its conventional, off-line counterparts any time soon. We certainly do not recommend that organizations drop their direct mail programs, telephone solicitation, charitable auctions, and face-to-face appeals because of the availability of raising funds via the Internet. But we do see using the Internet for fundraising as another tool in the fundraiser's toolbox, with its distinctive advantages and disadvantages, and as an attractive strategy to pursue.

With the advance of technology and creative business models advanced by third-party providers, even the smallest nonprofit can build and display a Web-based fundraising "public face" that will generate both funds and public support. The "playing field" has been leveled on the Internet. Even the smallest nonprofit can create a sophisticated Web site with e-philanthropy and e-commerce functions that has the look and feel of the largest nonprofits with full-time Webmasters. The price of entry into building a highly attractive, professional Web site for the typical nonprofit is a few dollars a month for a host and some sweat equity. There are many Web hosting services that will even provide free Web space for nonprofits. Free and moderately priced content management software makes Web site design and content updating a breeze for the expert and novice alike.

If you are not taking advantage of the Internet to raise funds for your organization, you are missing out on an opportunity to take your organization to the next level. It is not as hard to raise funds on the Internet as you might think. In Chapter 1, we will point out the advantages and disadvantages of online fundraising, discuss some of the issues involved in creating an online fundraising presence, and provide some practical advice for successful online fundraising. One major recommendation we offer is creating an online fundraising strategic plan, which we discuss in Chapter 2. Subsequent chapters give you a menu of components to include in this plan. You might consider revisiting Chapter 2 after you review the chapters on specific strategies that might be appropriate to include in your organization's plan.

So, let's get started!

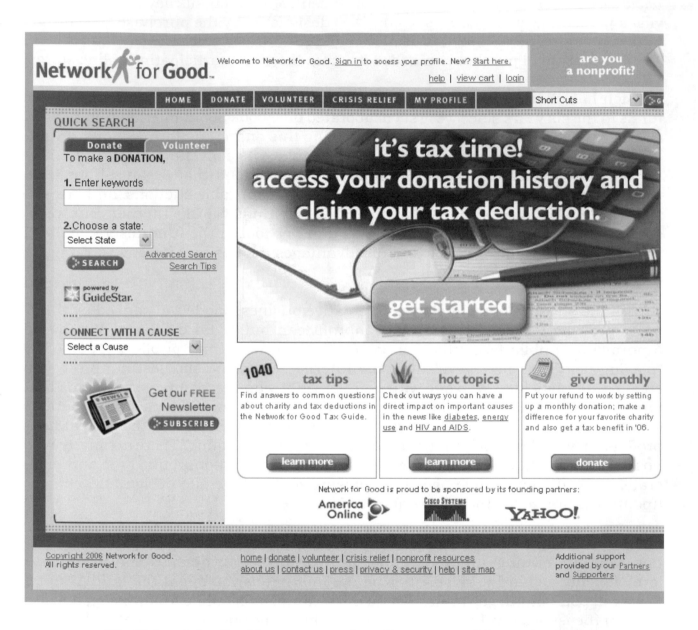

**The Network for Good home page at: http://www.networkforgood.org.
Reprinted with permission. See a review of this Web site on page 20.**

White Hat Communications

Chapter 1

Advantages and Disadvantages of Internet Fundraising

In putting together an online fundraising strategy, it is helpful to consider what makes online fundraising different from more conventional methods, such as direct mail, telephone solicitation, face-to-face meetings, and fundraising events. Doing so will permit you to take advantage of the strengths offered by online fundraising, and address how you will take into account its limitations.

Advantages of Internet Fundraising

Among the advantages are—

> 1. *The Internet has a systemized culture that offers potential donors an invitation to find your organization.*

Traditionally, nonprofit organizations reach out to potential donors by purchasing targeted mailing lists, advertising in print publications, and culling newspaper articles for information about those with substantial wealth for future follow-up communication. Through the use of links from other Web sites, search engines, online and print directories, and even word of mouth, potential donors will find your organization even if you have not found a way to contact them directly. Your organization can enhance this possibility by publicizing its Web site through news releases and other organizational communications and publications. See Chapter 7 for practical advice on attracting new visitors to your organization's Web site and keeping your visitors returning. The best such efforts lead donors to bookmark your site or link it to their personal home pages and blogs.

2. *There is almost universal access to the Internet and increasing comfort with online transactions.*

As we write this, more than 60% of American households have Internet access. Access in the office workplace has become almost universal with

Internet Fundraising Advantages:
• **donors find you** • **almost universal Internet access** • **24/7 accessibility** • **cost efficiencies** • **less intrusive and less annoying than other methods** • **decreased fundraising transaction processing costs** • **attractive models for partnering with for-profits**

more than 50 million Americans—37% of the total workforce—online at work, according to a report from eMarketer and *The Wall Street Journal*. According to a February 2003 study by Neilson-Netratings, more than a half-billion people worldwide are already connected to the Internet. Even those without their own computers have access to the Internet through their local schools and libraries, and free e-mail accounts are available to everyone with the motivation to sign up for one. People who only a few years ago didn't have an e-mail account eagerly participate in e-Bay auctions, purchase airline tickets and hotel rooms online, buy and sell securities, and examine PDF-format 990s online before they consider making a donation.

3. *Potential donors can make "contact" with your organization 24 hours a day, seven days a week from anywhere in the world for virtually no incremental cost on their part.*

Donors can find your Web site's "donate here" button at any time of the day or night from any computer that has a modem and access to a telephone line. Free or inexpensive software makes it practical for online forms to capture and process identifying information, payment information, and acknowledge a gift in the blink of an eye, providing the donor the instant gratification that is unavailable through many conventional fundraising methods. Compare making an online donation to the hassles of writing a check, filling out a paper form, finding a stamp and envelope, and taking the envelope to the post office. Or waiting for the organization's office to open in the morning to call in a pledge. By that time, your donor may have gone back to sleep and forgotten that he or she even wanted to make a donation.

4. *In many cases, raising money online is cheaper and faster than traditional fundraising methods.*

Compare making a change in a direct mail fundraising brochure to making the same change to the online brochure. Solicitation materials can be modified electronically at any time at virtually no cost, with no extra charges for color. Full-color, glossy brochures are often thrown away without having been read and are costly to update. Online fundraising messages can incorporate animations, scrolling messages, and flashing screens that make Web pages more dynamic than their print counterparts. These flashy bells and whistles can be added at no additional cost. In (almost) a blink of an eye and at virtually no cost, your computer can transmit thousands of electronic newsletters, each containing information of interest to your organization's supporters, as well as a subtle request for funds to finance a new service or program. There are no long distance charges, such as are incurred by a broadcast fax. Your telephones are not tied up if you use a Web-based service for this task. Responses (in the form of online donations) can literally come in within seconds, compared to the weeks required just to lay out and publish a print version of an organization's newsletter or fundraising brochure.

5. *The Internet is less intrusive and annoying than many conventional methods of fundraising.*

Direct mail and telephone solicitation appeals too often annoy and alienate. Both are getting less efficient: sending charitable bulk mail is getting more costly as a result of a postal rate increase that took effect in January 2006.

Telephone appeals are not as simple as in the past as a result of the popularity of "do-not-call" lists, caller ID, and other methods that potential donors use to screen calls from sources they do not know. To generate one donation from such a call, the organization must contact many individuals, most of whom will view your organization's contact as annoying.

Your fundraising message can be delivered by e-mail and read at a time that is convenient for the reader, who actually has signed up to receive it (along with other communications). While you won't want to send "spam" messages to ask for funds, there are several techniques you can use (see Chapter 4) that ethically and appropriately rely on e-mail to raise funds.

6. *Internet fundraising can easily be integrated with other marketing and promotional materials and programs.*

Solicitations for donations can be coordinated with other features of an organization's Web site, such as being included in an electronic newsletter, posted on donor recognition Web pages, on links to an organization's sales of goods and services, and with testimonials about the organization that indirectly enhance opportunities for giving. Individuals will visit your Web site for many reasons other than to make a donation. A functional Web site can plant the seeds of future giving and make it convenient for those who make spur-of-the-moment gifts based on what they see on your site.

7. *There are decreased transaction costs for Internet-based donation processing and donor outreach efforts.*

New business models make it easy to partner with third parties to streamline the online donation process and reach donors who otherwise might never have heard of the organization. Computers using sophisticated software automate many processes, such as accounting, database management, donor acknowledgment, and contact management, which previously relied on time-consuming work by staff. Many of these useful software packages can be purchased off the shelf, obviating the need to rely on third party providers.

8. *There are increased opportunities to build positive relationships with the business community.*

Many for-profit businesses are willing to sponsor the Web sites of charities, usually with no more than a "thank you" or a link (typically in the form of the sponsor's logo) from your site to the sponsor's own Web site. Internet models such as "click-to-give," online shopping malls, and charity portals are innovatively harnessing the power of the Internet to cement relationships between the business community and nonprofits that can carry over to relationships involving non-Internet collaborations.

Disadvantages of Internet Fundraising

Using the Internet for fundraising has its disadvantages, as well.

1. *The online medium can be impersonal compared to face-to-face fundraising.*

Online fundraising, with rare exceptions—such as when using real-time conferencing—is not face-to-face. The personal, human contact, with the ability to read, interpret, and respond to body language and other non-text cues, is an important component of fundraising, particularly when soliciting large gifts. There are limitations in relying on only what can be viewed on a computer screen to communicate.

2. Government regulation of online fundraising is unsettled.

There are unresolved legal and regulatory issues that have surfaced as a result of online fundraising. Among them are the degree to which the states regulate it, and what the roles are of third party for-profit dot-coms that agree to serve as intermediaries between donors and charities.

3. There are vulnerabilities as a result of having to rely on for-profit third parties.

Many charities are unwilling or unable to build the infrastructure to seek and process online donations. For-profit providers are available to offer these services (see Chapter 7). Many of them have no track record for reliability, ethical conduct, or financial stability. In addition, new business models have been created that involve partnerships and affiliation agreements with for-profits. The need for clear agreements between charities and these third parties raises issues of the transaction costs of creating contracts, motivation, opportunities for outright fraud, privacy with respect to sensitive donor and charity data, and the potential inability of a charity to control a third party's use of that charity's logo. Abuse by third party providers in the name of a charity can stain a reputation that took years to build. As we mentioned in our introduction, the PipeVine scandal of 2003 has placed a pall over relationships between charities and those who wish to help

> **Disadvantages of Internet Fundraising:**
>
> - **impersonal**
> - **unsettled regulatory climate**
> - **vulnerability to problems caused by working with outside parties**

them raise funds. That said, there are scores of reputable for-profit application service providers (ASPs) that have exemplary relationships with their nonprofit clients.

Most charities are recognizing that, in almost every case, the advantages of using the Internet to supplement traditional fundraising far outweigh the disadvantages. Almost every major charity in the United States has reported raising significant revenues utilizing the Internet. In the next chapters, we will describe some of the techniques charities are using to harness the power of the Internet, including use of e-mail, electronic newsletters, Web sites, online auctions, partnering with application service providers, networking with colleagues, online communities, using the Internet for prospect research, and finding funding sources on the Web.

Resources

The Foundation Center
http://fdncenter.org/

The Foundation Center is an independent nonprofit information clearinghouse established in 1956. The Center operates five libraries and provides materials to more than 200 public libraries. The mission of the organization is to foster public understanding of the foundation field by collecting, organizing, analyzing, and disseminating information on foundations, corporate giving, and related subjects. The site has a searchable archives, an excellent reference on how to prepare grant applications (*A Proposal Writing Short Course*, accessible from the *Learning Lab* menu on the home page), and standardized grant application forms. There is access to an online librarian who will answer your questions about where to find resources and basic information of interest to nonprofits. Just fill out the online form with your question. Under the "Learning Lab" menu on the home page, click on "topical research lists" and then "computer technology/nonprofit organizations and the Internet" for a list of print and online resources related to online fundraising.

Independent Sector
http://www.independentsector.org

Independent Sector is the leading advocacy coalition in Washington that serves the nonprofit sector. This site is the first place to go for definitive statistics of interest about the nonprofit sector (click on *Nonprofit Information Center*). It also has files on ethics, advocacy, accountability, and leadership issues. What makes this site particularly valuable to online fundraisers is current information about new laws and regulations affecting charities, as well as public policy advocacy updates.

Network For Good
http://www.networkforgood.org

Network for Good is a charity portal founded in November 2001 by AOL-Time Warner, Cisco Systems, and Yahoo!. Charities large and small can find extensive resources here to assist in their online fundraising efforts. Even more valuable is the service it provides to charities that register, enabling them to place a "donate here" link on their own Web pages to permit donors to make secure, online contributions without the charity needing its own merchant account. By 2004, Network for Good delivered $60 million to more than 15,000 charities. We applaud the sponsors for their vision in helping small charities build an infrastructure to accept real-time credit card donations and help even the smallest charity benefit from this service. From the site map *(http://www.networkforgood.org/sitemap/)*, view the files under "Working with Technology" for articles about online fundraising.

Nonprofit Managers' Library
http://www.mapnp.org/library/index.html

While much of this site is targeted to the needs of Minnesota nonprofits (such as local grant information), it is an excellent resource for all. The site boasts updated files on ethics, fundraising, communications skills, marketing, organizational change, risk management, strategic planning, and much more, sorted by 75 categories and indexed with 675 topics. There are numerous useful links to outside organizations that make this site an excellent resource for those interested in grants, foundations, government information, and general information useful to nonprofits. The site also hosts a free Nonprofit Organization and Management Development Program (a.k.a., *Free Nonprofit Micro-eMBA)*.

Nonprofit FAQ Resources for Fundraising Online
http://www.idealist.org

This site, first put online in 1994, is home to the popular Nonprofit FAQ, a searchable library of frequently asked questions (and answers) on nonprofit management, fundraising, technology, legal requirements, and almost every other practical facet of running a nonprofit organization. Bulletins are posted on the site with articles and late-breaking news of interest to the sector, and you can sign up to be notified by e-mail about newly available issues.

Tech Soup
http://www.techsoup.org

TechSoup *(http://www.techsoup.org)*, conceived and operated by CompuMentor, is a partnership of America Online, Novell, Microsoft, CNET, and several national and community foundations and other computer-related for-profits. Based in San Francisco, TechSoup has developed a reputation as being *the* place for nonprofits to visit for answers to questions about hardware and software, building Web sites, and taking advantage of all that technology can offer to help nonprofits achieve their vital missions. The content is all free and worthy of repeat visits. A service of TechSoup, TechSoup Stock, has distributed donated and discounted hardware and software from vendors such as Microsoft, Cisco, and Symantec. Overall, this is one of the best sites on the Internet for information about nonprofit technology issues, including hardware, software, connecting to the Internet, and finding discounts on products and services offered to nonprofit organizations. If there is something you want to do online and you don't have a clue about how to do it, come here first.

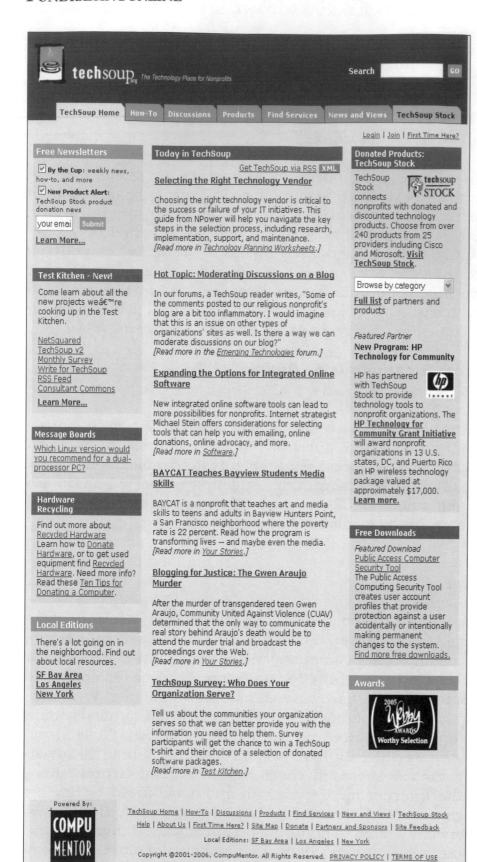

The Techsoup home page at: http://www.techsoup.org. Reprinted with permission. See a review of this Web site on page 21. Reprinted with permission.

Developing an Online Fundraising Strategic Plan

Why Nonprofit Organizations Need an Online Strategic Plan

The December 2004 tsunami disaster caught many international relief organizations unprepared for the outpouring of generosity from thousands of Americans and others who wanted to help and help soon. But some organizations had a written plan that prepared them to take quick action to use the Internet to maximum advantage. For example, within hours of the disaster, a handful of organizations purchased keywords on Google *(http://www.google.com)* so that individuals who searched on the term "tsunami" and related terms would see a link to pages that solicited donations for their relief efforts (see Chapter 6).

After the disastrous 2005 hurricane season, purchasing ads on the Google search engine became a perfunctory fundraising strategy. When we search on the keyword "Katrina," we find ads for organizations such as the International Red Cross, UNICEF, Save the Children, MercyCorps, Corps International, and Operation Blessing, in addition to many organizations that do *not* provide hurricane relief to the needy.

This particular strategy of search engine marketing paid off. Yet there were many issues that had to be decided in order to purchase the ads. Who would be responsible for creating the advertisement? Where would the funds come from to pay for it? How much should be invested? Who would be responsible for making sure that donations generated more than offset the costs, so a decision could be made to pull the ads if they weren't generating reasonable revenue? What other online fundraising strategies would be pursued when opportunities such as this arose? What other circumstances might arise, that could be planned for in advance, to mobilize the organization when there is a development that affects how the public perceives the organization or its mission?

Using a Strategic Approach

A strategic approach is valuable in creating the best possible coordination among online fundraising activities of an organization. For example, the direct marketing department wants to show the importance of many giving small gifts, while major gift staff want to demonstrate the powerful impact individuals can have. With careful planning, both points of view can be presented online in a balanced manner.

Similarly, are there strategies that could encourage donors to give through multiple philanthropic gateways (events, direct marketing, and so forth) rather than just steering donors to one or the other? Ensuring that donors can navigate seamlessly through the Web site is just as important as ensuring that each individual area appeals to its targeted audience. There are synergies across departments and programs that can only be captured if there is a coordinated and strategic approach to fundraising online.

> **Charities should:**
>
> - **develop a strategic Internet plan**
> - **have components in the plan to react to changing conditions**
> - **periodically evaluate their plans**

Engage in long term planning

Most large nonprofit organizations engage in long-term planning, and many develop formal strategic plans. These documents, often the culmination of months of work by staff, board, and other stakeholders, typically are a study of the organization's vision three to five years down the road. Considering advances in technology, changing markets, the effects of government cutbacks, and the emergence of competitors, the value of investing so much time and effort in developing an Internet strategic plan may seem dubious. Yet, long-term planning provides a forum to discuss issues in a proactive rather than a reactive mode. One benefit is that it can serve as a mandate to reallocate resources during a short-term emergency and consider issues during a time of relative calm rather than during the chaotic period that characterizes a time of crisis.

Regardless of whether an organization formalizes its online strategic plan or simply has a process to think about how it might respond to various environmental change scenarios, it is worth investing some time thinking about what the organization wants to accomplish with the new technology that facilitates online fundraising.

Who Puts the Plan Together

An organization's Internet fundraising strategy should not be decided piecemeal, but too often it is. Few organizations take the time to carefully plan, coordinate, integrate, and prioritize their online fundraising efforts. Instead, the approach is typically a kind of "evolution" in which one person or functional area, such as direct marketing, planned giving, or special events, implements an online approach that seems promising—even obviously necessary—for that particular person or area.

It is not uncommon for this to be advanced by a single front-line fundraiser who has a creative idea or talent, or who simply feels compelled to see his or her organization get out of the dark ages. The front line staff, however, is not always in the best position to shape the strategy of the organization. On the micro level, the ideas are often good ones and may largely be on target for where the organization should head, but these strategies need to reflect the broader goals and represent the commitments of the organization to truly create the strongest and most effective Internet fundraising approach.

Ensure top-down thinking

We feel that an organization's executive director should be the one to bring it all together and to ensure top-down thinking. By asking staff to produce an Internet fundraising strategic plan and participating hands-on, the executive director helps ensure that more than one person's input is involved and that broader buy-in is established—including that of the executive director himself or herself. The need to organize in this way may be particularly true for national groups with affiliates or chapters. But even an otherwise well integrated organization can fall into the trap in which the tail wags the dog, unless leadership is proactive.

One risk many organizations face when their online fundraising develops in a piecemeal way is that it shifts every time there is a staff change. Suppose, for example, that an organization is blessed with a fundraiser who has a talent and interest for maintaining a part of the organization's Web site for fundraising purposes. That fundraiser might develop a creative way for building and maintaining a donor stewardship and recognition program online. If that individual leaves, however, this feature may not be maintained by his or her successor. Will the next fundraiser have the skills necessary or the inclination to continue what his or her predecessor started? Unless there is a coordinated plan for the organization, to which the leadership is committed, then chances are that the answer is "no."

First, depending on the size of your organization, as an executive director, you should determine who to ask to write the plan and who will ultimately be responsible for monitoring its effectiveness in achieving your goals, fundraising or otherwise. This individual need not be a fundraiser, but must be someone who understands the overall organization. A knowledge of both fundraising and/or the technology will strengthen the ability to carry out this task, however.

What is In the Internet Strategic Plan

As you will find throughout this book, there are numerous possible approaches to online fundraising, each with many variations. The online activities that make sense for any organization will be very specific to that organization's needs. There is no one "right" way and no recipe for success. Deciding which fundraising approaches to pursue and how depends on largely subjective evaluations. Fundraisers often use their professional judgment and instincts to determine what will work for their particular cause, with their particular constituency, in their particular fundraising environment.

Those designated as strategic plan developers might begin by collecting input and ideas from fundraisers and other stakeholders. They need to ask fundraisers to brainstorm and detail the kinds of activities that they *could* do online, through the Web site or other means, to enhance their existing fundraising efforts (i.e., to be better planned gift, direct marketing, special events, or major gifts, fundraisers). Ultimately these online activities may affect their job descriptions, so at some point in the brainstorming process, staff need to be asked to reflect on the weaknesses, challenges, barriers, and conflicting priorities that may make some of the activities they list less attractive.

Using resources such as this book can help staff think creatively. In addition, staff can provide input on whether there are entirely new ways to generate revenue that strike them as being especially intriguing for the particular organization in question. These ideas will ultimately help leadership determine if there would be a benefit to creating a new position or new role. For example, if the organization determines that managing eBay charity auctions would be a valuable addition to its fundraising repertoire, then it may consider whether a volunteer opportunity or a new staff position needs to be created rather than adding a new responsibility to an existing position.

Once all of these ideas and their respective strengths/weaknesses are collected, then there needs to be a chance for the technology experts to add their input and to give realistic assessments of what can be done in-house versus hiring outside companies to manage. The time commitments need to be approximated as well as the hard costs. When this is done, then there should be an opportunity for leadership in other areas, programmatic and administrative, to comment on which ideas they think might create particular synergies and which are likely to cause potential conflicts.

If there are affiliate organizations, this process can naturally create special challenges, but an investment in the process could help to make the online fundraising a point in which the organization comes together—for the sake of its donor constituencies. At the same time, the process cannot drag out too long. A year of unnecessary delay in developing and implementing a plan may find that particular opportunities are lost to time or that its champion has left or lost enthusiasm. And what a difference a year makes when you consider the current pace of technological and cultural change!

A plan can, for this reason, have some ideas that are immediately and aggressively pursued in the short term, even if the overall package is still in development. This can help greatly in maintaining morale and even giving staff a chance to test ideas. Some activities that sound promising may prove to be more trouble than they are worth once they are tested.

An Internet strategic plan should answer some of the following questions, which we've categorized as those relating to leadership, the enhancement of existing efforts, new ideas, and practical implementation:

I. Leadership

- How much does the organization hope to raise through online fundraising compared to conventional efforts?
- How much is the organization willing to budget for online fundraising efforts?
- Should the organization hire staff specifically experienced in online fundraising?

II. Enhancing Existing Efforts

- What special events can be efficiently and effectively changed from offline to online to increase productivity and return on investment, and when should the transition occur?
- How will the organization use the Internet to enhance a new or existing capital campaign?
- What fundraising programs, such as tribute gifts, could benefit from online administration?

III. New Ideas

- When and how should the organization engage in Search Engine Marketing (SEM)?
- Should the organization engage in online charity auctions, and who will be responsible for coordinating them?
- Should the organization create an online community, and who will have the responsibility to maintain it?

IV. Practical Implementation Questions

- Who is responsible for updating the online fundraising Web pages?
- What training will be provided to staff to upgrade their online fundraising skills?
- Who will monitor government regulation of online fundraising?
- Who will update the plan?
- Who will evaluate whether efforts included in the plan are successful?
- Under what circumstances will the organization engage the services of application service providers to assist in online fundraising efforts, and what process will be required to hire such outside consultants?

Prioritizing Components of the Plan

Equally as important is the question of prioritization. Because there are so many ideas for enhancing fundraising online or creating new Internet-based sources of revenues, one must start with the realization that no organization can pursue them all. Thought must be given to what directions the organization wishes to take. The question should not be, "Does this idea generate net revenue or benefit fundraising?" The question is instead, "Does this idea fit into our overall priorities and capacities, and how does it compare to other options?" The plan needs to also consider potential unintended consequences of each strategy, such as how each planned strategy might adversely affect other departments, programs, and activities.

The thinking is much the same as any other functional area. No organization wants to pursue every possible form of special event. A car wash might generate revenue, but many organizations would reject organizing one if it isn't deemed the best use of a fundraiser's time or the right fit for the character of the organization. This applies to Internet fundraising strategies, as well.

Again, the problem is that without leadership, staff members will often take the initiative themselves, and while being proactive is admirable, it may lead to disjointed approaches that may over time make the organization look sloppy to its constituency.

Time Constraints, Resources, and Goals

The Internet strategic plan needs not only to have concrete strategies to increase online fundraising (e.g., "hold an online charity auction"), but also to make it clear when this strategy will be implemented ("by July 2008") and the goal that is sought ("that will raise at least $25,000 in net revenue for the organization"). It should be clear who on the staff is the key person responsible for implementing the particular strategy, what support staff will be expected to assist, and what resources will be allocated for each particular effort.

The fundraising team (and perhaps other key stakeholders) needs to be involved throughout the process. Fundraisers cannot have online responsibilities foisted on them, or they will not make it work. Whoever is charged with writing the plan needs to see himself or herself as a facilitator—trying to guide the team toward a cohesive and well-integrated approach. But first and foremost is maintaining enthusiasm. Those implementing an online fundraising strategy, and responsible for its success, have to own the ideas.

They also have to see that the organization is committed to them, as well. Knowing that their preferred approaches are part of the plan (even if tweaked to fit the organization's needs) ensures fundraising staff that they are truly creating change and influencing the direction of the organization.

As suggested, the plan should articulate the goals—most of which have been provided directly from the fundraisers. And it should set out how these goals will be monitored over time. Overall monitoring is often lost in the piecemeal approach, as totals raised get merged in to like gifts given offline. While gifts must be counted according to their functional type, some system of tracking online giving in each area is also important and will help the strategic plan develop and keep up over time.

Finally, the strategic plan needs to maintain a good balance between firmly and confidently setting a course of action and also being flexible to accommodate a rapidly changing environment. Donors should not see the Web site's fundraising areas changing every year. Staff do not want to put a lot of work into something that is no longer online a year later. At the same time, as we all know, the Internet is constantly changing and new technologies are created every day, many of which can affect nonprofit fundraising.

Evaluating the Plan

A smart organization will not only monitor the effectiveness of its Internet plan each year (or quarter), but it will also reevaluate it regularly. It can do this by inviting qualitative feedback from staff each year. In addition to knowing how many dollars the online giving forms brought in or how many major donors have interfaced with the Web site, the organization should ask staff all the time, "Is this the best approach? Are there things you wish we could do differently? What are our competitors doing? What does our technology staff say is possible these days?"

In summary, many of the same reasons apply for making a strategic plan for Internet fundraising as for any area of an organization's operation. The most successful nonprofits will utilize such thinking in this area to maximize their success in online fundraising.

Resources

Free Management Library's On-Line Nonprofit Organization Development Program Module #9: Basics in Developing Your Fundraising Plan
http://www.managementhelp.org/np_progs/fnd_mod/fnd_raise.htm

Included on this site are links to articles about what you can do to raise funds online. Although many of the articles appear to be from just before the turn of the century, these resources still provide a good overview of the benefits of harnessing the Internet for online fundraising.

The Nonprofit GENIE
http://www.genie.org

This site is a project of the California Management Assistance Partnership. Here you can find book reviews of nonprofit management books, plus 158 entries in a comprehensive Frequently Asked Questions (FAQ) for nonprofit managers (undergoing extensive renovations when this review was carried out in January 2006), organized in nine general categories, such as insurance and strategic planning. There are plenty of interesting links to nonprofit resources, as well.

Nonprofit Good Practice Guide
http://www.npgoodpractice.org/

This site is a project of The Dorothy A. Johnson Center for Philanthropy & Nonprofit Leadership at Grand Valley State University. The searchable site is organized by 10 topic areas, including "Fundraising and Financial Sustainability" and "Technology." You can find links to more than 4,300 articles, online courses (many of which are free), research papers, booklets, and case studies, all organized by topic. While the strength of this site is in its organization of links to online resources found on other Web sites, it does have substantial useful content of its own. The *Guide* has a unique way of integrating both types of resources in a pleasing format that is both fun to browse and almost guaranteed to uncover some useful nugget that is worthwhile to print and save. Clicking on each topic area takes you to a page that opens with a list of "preferred practices" and "pitfalls"—in short, a list of "do's" and "don'ts." While many of these initial offerings have been seeded by the center's seasoned executive director, Joel Orosz, Ph.D., there is a link that permits visitors to add to the lists, and to also submit information about new resources. Thus, the site is organic, and is likely to become one of the leading sources nonprofit staff and board members can turn to for advice once folks know it is available and it reaches the critical mass necessary to sustain itself as an online community. Another useful feature is a glossary, accessible from the home page menu. It defines almost 3,000 terms of interest to nonprofit organizations, some with hyperlinks that point your browser to supplemental information. All in all, this is one of the best new resources on the Internet for nonprofit organizations.

Online Fundraising Resources Center
http://www.fund-online.com/musings/index.html

This collection of essays by Adam Corson-Finnerty and Laura Blanchard is a fascinating and well-written look at e-philanthropy. Many are based on their postings to the Cybergifts electronic mailing list. The site includes teaching materials from classes and presentations, and chapters from the CD companion to their book *Fundraising and Friend-Raising on the Web*.

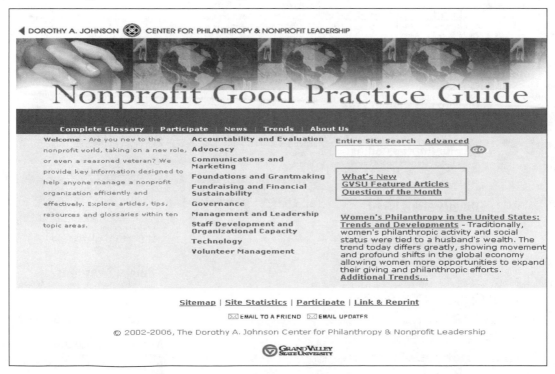

The Nonprofit Good Practice Guide home page at: http://www.npgoodpractice.org. Reprinted with permission. See a review of this Web site, a service of Grand Valley State University, on page 30.

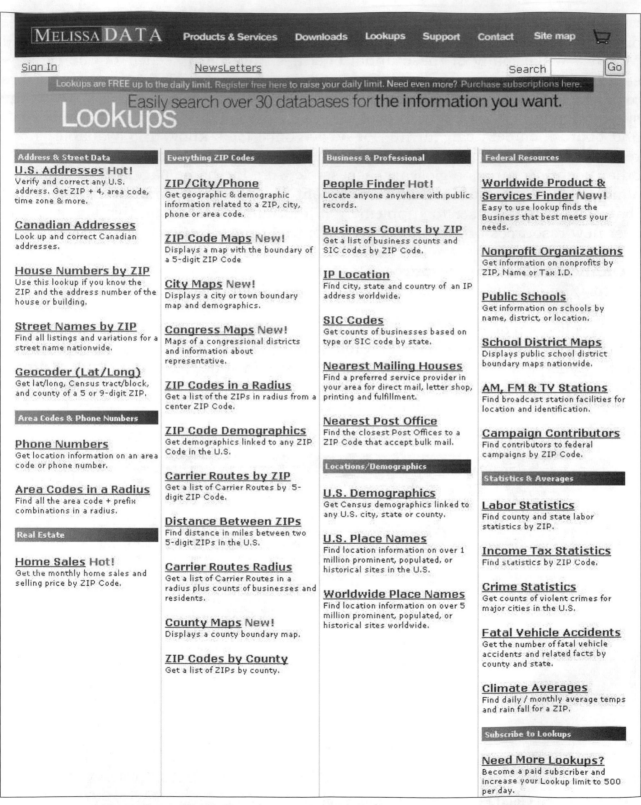

The Melissa Data Lookups page at: http://www.melissadata.com/lookups. Reprinted with permission. See a review of this Web page on page 56.

Chapter 3

How Fundraising Professionals Are Harnessing the Internet

In this chapter, we will explore how the Internet is being used to enhance existing nonprofit fundraising techniques by staff who have principal responsibility for direct marketing, online auctions, prospect research, major gifts, corporate donations, foundation donations, special events, and capital campaigns.

Most organizations do not dedicate staff solely to Internet fundraising. Instead, most development teams are integrating Internet approaches into their existing fundraising programs. So the question for these organizations is not necessarily, "How can I raise support online?" The more particular question may be "How can the Internet enhance our annual appeals, our major gift program, our fundraising events, and our capital campaigns?"

Direct Marketing

Organizations of all types utilize basic direct marketing to reach the broadest possible public for support. Through mailing campaigns, these organizations strive to gain vital revenue to maintain their operations. The goals of a direct marketing effort are to build a mailing list as large as possible, as engaged as possible, and abundant with the names and addresses of those who support loyally, often in unrestricted dollars.

The challenges posed by direct marketing are ideally addressed by Web-based efforts. First, the Web provides a cost-effective way to help the public know about the organization. For large national organizations, a Web presence is absolutely vital and most likely to result in people seeking and finding their way to the organization. But even on the local level, a Web presence will lead to results.

The Community Food Bank (CFB) in Tucson, Arizona *(http://www.communityfoodbank.org/)* set up its Web site hoping that the local community would learn about what it was trying to do and support its efforts. Although it took six months, the organization began seeing donations coming in every day through its Web site. A year later, donations of up to $1,000 were given regularly online.

Attract new donors

Direct marketing online may also attract a different kind of donor. The Community Food Bank was used to receiving support primarily from those over 50 giving through traditional direct marketing efforts. A survey of the organization's new online constituency demonstrated a dramatic increase in donors who were in their 30s and 40s. This younger contributor was being engaged for the first time thanks simply to an Internet marketing approach.

> **Direct marketing has long been a key tool for fundraisers. The Internet offers unique advantages in direct marketing, allowing you to—**
> - **attract new donors**
> - **build the giving "habit"**
> - **cultivate a community of donors**
> - **make giving easy**
> - **integrate and reinforce traditional direct appeals**
> - **engage donors in the organization**

Build the giving "habit"

Web sites as a form of direct marketing are also credited for larger and repeated giving. Consider that most donors who respond to annual solicitations or direct marketing appeals give according to their income level. This contrasts with major donors, who give based on their assets. The size of an annual gift is based on disposable funds after meeting one's spending and saving needs at the time. When a gift is made only once each year, then the organization may only receive the contribution the person can afford in the particular month when the gift is made. Donors who give monthly will therefore tend to give larger gifts than those who give once in a year. Most donors do not save their disposable income each month in order to preserve their ability to give the largest contribution over the course of the year.

Promote monthly giving habits

For this reason, many organizations are seeing the value in promoting monthly giving habits. Donors who click to give often develop such habits. This is likely to be an especially effective mechanism for churches and temples to which contributions are often made in the form of monthly or weekly gifts. An online appeal may make it easier, especially for individuals who miss attending services in a given week. Any organization, however, that hopes to increase repeat giving will be served well by offering Web site giving options consistent with this approach.

Although monthly giving helps individuals maximize their philanthropy to organizations they care about, it is inconvenient to write a check that often. It requires time, stamps, and envelopes, and if any one of those is missing when the donor is ready to give, then the donor may not send the gift at all that month. Some organizations attempt to encourage frequent giving by mailing more often or soliciting pledges to be paid monthly and providing the materials to make the gift, but this is costly and may not appeal to all donors who are already inundated by mail.

Giving online addresses all of these concerns. It allows monthly giving habits to form without the inconveniences. Increasingly, people are getting used to paying their monthly bills online. Many donors are willing to support organizations in the same manner. Giving donors the option to automate giving or to give monthly shows that the organization is service oriented.

Cultivate a community of donors

Another aspect of Web-based direct marketing is the opportunity to cultivate a relationship with a large constituency. Direct marketers know that engagement is necessary to maintain their constituency's support over time. At a minimum, organizations need to communicate with donors and engage them in a participatory way. Personalization is important as organizations seek to build a real relationship with their donor public.

Conveying information can be a challenge if carried out primarily through direct marketing appeals. Letters and brochures convey only so much information. As a result, most are drafted to the needs of the largest segment of the donor public. A shotgun approach is necessary for effective fundraising. Thus, for example, if an environmental organization expects that the majority of its donors are more moved by hearing about its latest advocacy efforts than they are by learning about environmental impact research, then its appeals will likely focus on the former and neglect the latter. It's simply impractical to appeal to the smaller segments of the organization's constituency. A Web site, however, allows visitors to go to whatever topic interests (and moves) them, and these visitors can be invited to contribute while there.

Make giving easy

Several direct marketing fundraisers shared that online fundraising reduced barriers to giving. They advised us to **make sure the option to give is pervasive in your site.** The button to make a donation should exist on every page. Donors should not be required to leave what they are reading to navigate your site in order to find the place where a gift can be made. When possible, fundraisers can also relate the value of giving right at that point. How would $50 help advance the advocacy efforts of the organization? How would the same gift affect vital research supporting the cause?

Integrate and reinforce traditional direct appeals

Another helpful technique is to integrate mailings, phone appeals, and print ad forms of direct marketing with the organization's Web site. Repetition is often valuable in direct marketing. One message is easily missed. A letter can be tossed out because it is received at an inconvenient time. The Web site is a place where the same message can be viewed just because it's available when the donor wants to read it— even if that's at 3 a.m. Repetition helps to ensure that the message is seen.

Repetition may also strengthen the message. Seeing an image online that was previously seen in a magazine ad or reading a story that was heard in a phone call reinforces the message. The organization looks well organized and lively when something received in another medium is carried through online. This can demonstrate that the Web site is being maintained daily, consistently with other communications. Not everyone reads the "last updated" line to determine this.

One organization we spoke with tracks the relationship between its traditional media approaches and the Web site. A mailing, for example, will often refer the donor public to a particular place within the organization's Web site. The resulting traffic to that page can be tracked as another way to test the reaction to the mailing. From there, similar tracking can be done to determine if donors are then going to the donations page and making a gift. Over time, such research can be essential to perfecting a direct marketing approach to fundraising.

Engage donors in the organization

Communicating effectively with donors will help increase giving, but actively engaging donors can truly raise the bar on contributions. In an e-mail newsletter, the Brookfield Zoo offered recipients the chance to name the latest zoo baby. This kind of participation encourages individuals to click from the e-mail to the Web site and feel as if they are actively participating in the life of the organization.

The zoo's engagement, however, began earlier when individuals first opted to receive the e-mail newsletter (see Chapter 4). Giving people the chance to opt in is a major tool for direct marketing fundraisers. By opting in, the subscriber gives an organization permission to write (and to solicit). This is familiar to many membership organizations, universities, and clubs. Such organizations have long benefited from the bond their constituency has agreed to accept from the start. Other organizations have been disadvantaged by inherently temporary, arms-length, one-sided relationships. If donors send checks in response to a direct mail appeal, they are not necessarily going to view themselves as a part of that organization in the long term. But if they ask to receive communications online, they may do so—especially if the organization takes the opportunity to create a personalized and welcoming environment.

Establish a bond with discussion forums

Donor discussion forums are another form of engagement. They can help a constituency establish a bond with the organization and a relationship for appeals that feel more individualized.

Dads and Daughters *(http://www.dadsanddaughters.org/),* for example, is an organization that has grown

> *Fundraising tip:* E-mail communications have a different tone. As one direct marketing manager shared, Web sites are all about the organization. The tone is focused on "we." Mail appeals, however, tend to start with "you," the donor. They bring the donor into the heart of the organization and reinforce the idea that the recipients are being asked to support "their" mission through "their" organization. Communications by e-mail, whether solicitations or not, should similarly focus on the donor.

around an opt-in discussion forum. DADS seeks to help fathers be successful parents for their daughters and engages them in addressing cultural and commercial messages that may negatively affect girls or damage their self-esteem. From the first page, visitors are encouraged to sign up for the electronic mailing list. The e-mail discussions are two-way. Participants can raise everyday parenting challenges and get input from other members. E-mail action alerts are sent to the list, as well as requests for support—from financial to in-kind needs. This works because each person has opted in and feels sufficiently engaged, so the requests for support are viewed as appropriate, even welcomed as convenient.

This approach is obviously more challenging for larger, well-established organizations, but any degree of engagement of one's donor public can enhance the level of giving, the frequency, and donor loyalty.

Even the simple act of registering at a site can create some level of engagement. Some organizations will encourage Web site visitors to register. Then when they return and "sign in," they get a degree of personalization from the site itself. Beginning with a "welcome back Mary" sign, the site can also be made to recognize various preferences or past activities. Online message boards, for example, may show what has been read and what has not.

Password protect the site

Having a password into a Web site encourages visitors to bookmark the site. By registering visitors, an organization can also request information. Visitors may voluntarily share a range of data on their interests, their contact information, including phone number, and even wealth information. Some organizations will retain credit card information with confidentiality. This can be done to make it even easier to give regularly. Donors don't even have to take their cards from their wallet or purse.

Prospect Research

Prospect research includes finding information not only on individuals, but also on corporate and private foundations and government agencies that will provide funds. It encompasses collecting and analyzing information to help fundraisers find out the ability and inclination of prospective donors to donate, and obtaining clues to the best strategy to assist donors in providing the largest gift that would feel comfortable to them. Good prospect research cannot guarantee successful "asks," but it can provide critical information about the background, needs, style, financial capacity, approachability, and interests of someone who can make or break your fundraising campaign. Before the Internet revolution, prospect researchers used newspapers and magazines, real estate records, data and mailing lists purchased from private companies or other charities, annual reports from businesses, industry association directories, and biographical directories (such as *Who's Who in America)* to cull for juicy leads. Today, there is a plethora of electronic sources, many free, dwarfing those available a decade ago.

> **Prospect researchers use the Internet to—**
> - **identify potential donors**
> - **find out about the interests, motivations, and backgrounds of potential donors**
> - **assess the financial capacity of potential donors**
> - **cull for tidbits of information that can be helpful in crafting a successful "ask"**

Treat $50 donors today like they will be $50 million donors tomorrow

One cannot ever know when any particular $50 donor today may become a potential $50 million donor tomorrow, and thus it is important to treat every donor and potential donor as if his or her donation is the most important the organization will ever receive. Yet the mathematics are that a single $5 million donation has as much purchasing power as 100,000 donations of $50 each, and with a lot less transaction cost. No wonder charities are willing to make substantial investments in prospect research.

Find prospects using free online databases

When Gary Grobman speaks at conferences making his PowerPoint presentations on the subject of online fundraising, one prospect research technique never fails to leave his audience ooohing and aaahing. He points his Web browser to *http://www.melissadata.com/lookups.* Then he clicks on "Campaign Contributors." Then he asks a fundraiser in the audience to provide him with a 5-digit ZIP-code of an upscale neighborhood in the area of his or her charity. When Gary submits that into the online form, it returns information about individuals who made contributions of at least $200 to a federal election campaign. Inevitably, the list is a "who's who" of philanthropists. It doesn't take much imagination to think about how such a database can be of use to fundraisers. Other sites that are favorites of professional prospect researchers include Edgar Online People *(http://access.edgar-online.com/people/peopleSearch.asp),* Hoover's Online *(http://hoovweb.hoovers.com/free/),* Forbes.com *(http://www.forbes.com/),* and David Lamb's Prospect Research Page *(http://www.lambresearch.com/).* Some of these sites are free; others require a subscription.

> **Tips on "Googling"**
>
> - don't neglect other search engines.
> - use other "names" for the person, such as nicknames, abbreviations and diminutives (e.g. "Bob" instead of Robert").
> - search on the names of close family members.
> - remember that many entries are duplicative; practice skimming, so you can assess the value of 50,000 "hits" in a Google search quickly and get the gist of the information available using the search engine.

Identify interests, motivations, backgrounds, and financial capacity

In 2003, Jerold Panas wrote a riveting two-part column in *Contributions* Magazine about his harrowing, semi-successful experience in making a $50 million "ask" on behalf of a university fundraising campaign. Obviously, the preparation required for such an endeavor is more than, let's say, seeking a $50 donation, because the stakes are so much higher. Veteran fundraiser and *Washington Post* columnist Bob Levey often tells the story of a neophyte fundraiser who approached the legendary philanthropist and *Washington Post* owner Katherine Graham seeking a major gift for a worthy cause, only to be immediately shown the door after calling her "Katie."

Major gift officers and other high-level fundraising and executive staff want to know their prospects. They want to understand their potential so they can make realistic assessments for future solicitations. They want to understand their personalities so they can approach them in the right way. They want to learn their motivations so they can focus on what appeals to each particular individual and avoid pitfalls that might turn them off to the organization. They want ideas for making initial introductions.

The Internet offers an efficient tool to access lots of publicly available information about individuals, careful online research can answer many questions about potential donors.

Major Gifts

Major gift fundraisers work closely with a small set of an organization's top donors. Their donors contrast with annual supporters in making "stop and think" contributions ranging from once every few years to once in a lifetime. Major gifts tend to be given for special purposes—often restricted to projects with specific measurable outcomes. How do the Internet and the organization's Web site and electronic communications assist the major gifts team?

Don't use the Internet as a crutch

Fundraisers often view the Internet with great hope for finding the key information and insight they feel they need. The reality is that the Internet can be useful, but ought not be used as a crutch. For the most part, prospect research should be left to prospect researchers (if your organization has them), particularly for determining giving capacity. While many cannot help but "Google" a prospect before a visit or while planning an initial contact, fundraisers should be careful not to rely too heavily on cursory research or believe that they can truly understand the person from whatever they find. Major gift work still requires the traditional emphasis on face-to-face interactions for getting to know one's prospects and building a real relationship.

> **Major gifts officers—**
>
> - **need ideas for making initial introductions**
> - **use the Internet to keep abreast of the latest philanthropic-related news**
> - **use the Internet to communicate information to major donors and prospective major donors**
> - **use custom-designed pages to communicate the benefits of making major gifts**

In addition to aiding in prospect research, the Internet can be a valuable aid in all aspects of major gift fundraising, from identifying new donors, to cultivating relationships, to solicitation and stewardship.

Find hidden potential donors using the Internet

Identifying major gifts donors is one of a fundraiser's greatest challenges. Few donor prospects contact an organization requesting to have their relationships with the organization managed by a major gifts officer. Instead, they are often initially hidden. They may be hidden in the public at large, interested in the mission of your organization, but not yet connected. Or they may be hidden among the current annual donors. Some of the wealthiest individuals still give $25 or $50 gifts in response to direct mail appeals.

Sharing philanthropic news within your organization can also be an effective way to help encourage those who support far below their capacity to perhaps step forward and give more. Major gift stories provide a wonderful opportunity to communicate not only about the programs of the organization, but about the exciting support and endorsement a major gift demonstrates. To the extent possible, major gifts fundraisers want these stories to be shared broadly to set the highest possible bar on generous giving and to build a stronger culture of philanthropy throughout their donor constituency.

As you identify major donor prospects, the next step is to begin building a stronger affinity with the organization. This can mean several things, each of which may be enhanced through Internet tools.

Fundraising tip: *An element that may help in cultivating prospect relationships is to have a staff directory at your Web site, preferably including pictures. For one thing, just as major gifts officers want to be able to read something about their donors and prospects, donors may want to investigate your leadership. Giving a bio online can help them do this.*

Educate major donors about the organization

Potential major donors need to get to know the organization and its mission over time. There is an education process that must happen. While the most important efforts will be face-to-face, you can enhance these interactions and develop a closer connection through e-mail communications and referring donors to specific parts of your Web site. E-mail takes on a very different nature when the recipient knows the sender. If you are managing the fundraising for a political campaign, for example, and you tell a particular donor that the candidate will e-mail directly with some information, this is quite different from getting a general letter from the candidate to a larger number of people.

In short, e-mail can be a convenient form of communication but also extremely personal if it is combined with other one-on-one approaches. A fundraiser might send a note referencing a particular topic or article on your Web site for which they know the donor has interest. Fundraisers can facilitate communications with board members, leaders, and others as they help the donor understand how they operate and work to accomplish their goals. You might even have a program beneficiary write to a prospective donor to share information about the impact the organization has had.

If your organization has developed good case materials, you may want to adopt the common practice among successful fundraising programs of including case statements online in PDF format. You can see numerous samples of these simply by entering "case statement" into any popular search engine, or check the samples posted at:

http://dukehealth1.org/childrens_services/case_statement_p2.asp
and
http://www.capitalcampaigns.com/sampcasehosp1.html

In addition to educating a donor about your organization, fundraisers need to listen to major gift prospects and understand their needs, interests, and motivations. Again, the addition of Internet communication into the traditional mix can help escalate input both ways.

Keep track of the relationship between donors and the organization

Similarly, major gift donors and prospects often need to develop a relationship with leadership and trust in their ability to guide the organization successfully. Enhancing face-to-face relationships through online communications can increase the leadership's ability to engage with prospects. Your organization's leader can interact with higher quality communications as well as with a greater quantity of donors. Major gifts fundraisers should actively recommend, draft, and track e-mail conversations between leadership and top prospects.

Leadership should also remember to share valuable discussions with individuals who are supporting the organization. Remember to send a blind copy to relevant staff. Private conversations should be respected, but when appropriate, sharing information can avoid duplication of efforts or wasted time later.

Include contact information on the Web site

Although you may have given a donor prospect your card, it is common for anyone to misplace a number and seek you out through your Web site. Web sites that lack simple staff directories can create frustrations, and visitors may feel that you have failed to focus on helping them navigate your organization. With a staff directory, a donor will gain a more positive impression. Being able to "see" the staff they are trying to find will help make the communications seem more personal, warm, and friendly.

Ultimately, major gifts work leads to solicitations. Here your Web site can again support your efforts, beginning by detailing your organization's giving opportunities. Whether or not you have a case statement online, you should also detail major gift projects that can be funded. Because major donors tend to need specificity, it may be wise to give substantial details. Rather than just mentioning the organization's top giving levels, you can provide a description of how the organization can use gifts of $25,000 or $100,000 or $1 million. Your description can provide the impact, the visibility to the donor, and the reason why these opportunities are so high a priority.

Develop Web pages that encourage major gifts

While it may be unlikely that a donor will randomly visit your site and contact you interested in one of your top giving opportunities, the presence of these at the Web site can support gift discussions. Keeping these online reaffirms for donors that they authentically do represent the organization's top priorities. And you never know when your organization will receive a donation windfall as a result.

In addition to presenting top gift opportunities online, you should also detail giving vehicles. Many organizations provide some information about planned giving options, estate gifts, and instructions for giving stock gifts or mutual funds. Such practical information can help donors as they consider making major contributions. Try to ensure that your site has all the details a donor would need and up-to-date contact information in case they have questions.

Here are some examples of such pages:

American Red Cross (http://www.redcrosslegacy.org)
National Foundation for Infectious Diseases (http://www.nfid.org/docs/donations/planned/)
Harvard Alumni (http://www.haa.harvard.edu/pgo/)

In presenting both giving opportunities and giving vehicles, what can be particularly helpful are actual donor demonstrations. If donors are willing, you can share their stories as models for others. Major donors often are pleased to do this, because it ensures that their leadership gift is actually leading. Suppose you wish to show what a charitable gift annuity can do for a donor. While you probably don't want to share the exact financial details of any individual donor's gift annuity, you can still articulate and quote a donor to demonstrate why such gifts can be mutually advantageous.

The same can be done for giving options—adding a personal touch to your list of giving opportunities. In this way, you gain the endorsement of past donors to promote new major gift philanthropy. Donors might be asked to share what motivated them to make the gift. They can share their appreciation for the visibility or the chance a gift gave them to remember a loved one. They can articulate the impact they have seen their gift have and how that made them feel. All of this can make a significant difference to a new donor. It will also add value and interesting reading to the giving opportunities section, so you may have better reason to direct donors there.

Post donor recognition pages

Once you have secured a major gift, stewardship and recognition come into play. Here there are many options, and organizations may want to think through it carefully. There is no substantial research on the risks/benefits of recognizing gifts online. Some fundraisers are hesitant. Even if donors approve, they may worry about getting unwanted attention by being put online for their major gift. Organizations may worry that other organizations will fish for the recognition pages and immediately try to "steal away" their donors.

Others are more optimistic and see more value in the gains that publicizing a gift online can have. As we review these options, we leave it to the reader to weigh the pros and cons.

One method of recognizing gifts is to create an online donor board. Many organizations provide donor boards in their buildings, especially museums, universities, theaters, and other places that have high visitor traffic. Donors appreciate donor boards, because they provide visible recognition. Organizations enjoy the opportunity to encourage other gifts. Because Web sites often attract substantial visibility, an online board may be desirable. We may even see more of these in the future, in particular from organizations that do not have a suitable or sufficiently visible location for a traditional donor board.

> **The Internet can be used to automate many time-consuming tasks relating to special events work, including—**
>
> - **publicizing events and their schedules**
> - **recruiting volunteers and donors**
> - **registering participants**
> - **recognizing participants**
> - **making the event planning and post event celebration interactive**

Consider posting virtual donor plaques

If an organization is concerned that listing donor names on a donor board may lead to other competing organizations tapping into their donor constituency, it may consider using graphical donor "plaques" instead of a text list. A graphical plaque is even more attractive. It would mean that you put the donor's name on an image that appears like a real-life plaque. As an image, it cannot be found by regular search engine methods, provided that the donor's name is not used as the name of the image file.

A more detailed possibility for donor recognition is to build pages dedicated to donors. These can contain some combination of background on individuals and their families, and the programs they are funding. Such pages can be done in combination with a donor board, allowing individuals to click on the name for more information. Donor boards and donor pages offer the possibility for greater visibility and may make donors feel a greater sense of how they are creating a legacy for the organization.

A variation on this is the online press release. Oftentimes, donors hope for a press release in response to their gifts. Unfortunately, most newspapers and media outlets are not interested in pure philanthropic stories, short of the mega-gifts that happen from time to time. But a formal press release can be posted online and made visible to those visiting the Web site. While perhaps not as exciting as being in the *New York Times,* such visibility can at least be a practical compromise solution.

Again—be very careful to communicate with every donor as you do anything with his or her name online. Even seemingly harmless forms of recognition, such as attaching a name to a professorship or a program detailed online may upset a donor. Communicating in advance is necessary.

Special Events

A museum organizes an annual gala event. A health organization holds an annual bike-a-thon. A university seeks class gifts in preparation for its big reunion weekend. A political campaign organizes "meet up" events to raise money. A church group plans a concert to raise support.

Events, although all very different, are a mainstay in the fundraising menu of most every kind of nonprofit organization. But what does this have to do with the Internet? How can the Internet enhance such programs? How can it help them have a bigger impact? How can it help them grow over time? How can it help them attract larger numbers of people? How can it help increase their visibility?

Most special events fundraisers see their role as two-fold. First, they want to raise significant support for their organization while controlling costs. The second objective of special events is to create awareness and visibility for the organization. For this reason, gala events may be lavish affairs.

Increase visibility for your special event

Visibility as an objective serves multiple purposes. Walks, galas, and other high profile events, for example, have helped to educate and make the public more aware of devastating diseases, to move the government to support programs for the poor, and to build excitement about cultural events. Such events have direct mission benefits.

In addition, visibility can serve other fundraising goals. Fundraising events can help to identify new major gift donors or to recognize existing ones. They offer a special visible option for recognizing corporate philanthropy. They provide an opportunity to address a larger donor constituency and to build their knowledge of and commitment to the organization.

Attract corporate sponsorship with similar markets

Understanding the complex goals of a special event fundraiser, we can begin to look at how the Internet might be helpful. Let's focus first on corporate event sponsorship. Highly visible special events provide an opportunity to link corporations to philanthropy in a context that is often particularly valued by the company. If a company has a market that is similar to your organization's beneficiary public, then it may be particularly attracted to event sponsorship.

Events covered by the media often acknowledge such philanthropy in a way they never would otherwise. Outright major gifts almost never get major publicity, unless they are extremely large, i.e., in excess of $25 million. But the news will often show a corporate check presentation as small as $10,000, if it is done in the context of a public event of interest.

Develop a page for your special event

As fundraisers look for and approach potential event sponsors, the more visibility they can offer them, the more appealing their proposal will be. Using the organization's Internet site to show how the sponsor's name will be featured is one valuable part of that package, particularly for organizations with heavy traffic. This can be done on a special page dedicated to the event, but linked from the organization's home page. Doing the same in mass e-mail communication to the organization's constituency about the event can be another aspect of this.

Is there value to a special page dedicated to an event like a gala? The short answer is "absolutely!" A page (or section) on a major event gives a fundraiser a chance to create an ongoing album for the event. It should contain photos of the most recent event, as well as substantive information about what the event is accomplishing. Over time, archived pages can be kept at the site, so visitors can look back to years past. A section of the Web site dedicated to a signature event can be a great point of pride for an organization and for its constituency as the program grows.

First time attendees will have a sense of the event if they visit the page. Individuals may encourage others to purchase seats or tables and may point friends to your site for this information. Previous attendees will enjoy seeing their own pictures there. Donors and sponsors may link to this part of your site.

Over the long-run, an Internet presence for a major gala event can enhance the program. It can create loyalty in those who have attended in the past and help to broaden the appeal of the event significantly. The gala page can celebrate the visibility achieved each year—linking to news coverage it received.

Put the gala program booklet online

Ultimately, this will all serve to help raise the fundraising sights for a gala style event. Donors can give through the gala site. Individuals who cannot attend the event might especially enjoy being part of the fundraising action in this way. Some organizations may wish to put their program booklet online and raise the price for a page by adding an Internet version of the space in addition to the printed version. Auction items not purchased at the event can be auctioned off after the event, via the Web site.

In short, the Internet gala page can bring a major event to life *before* and help keep the excitement going *after* the actual event itself. As participants feel a part of the site through the images and perhaps the words they add there, they will feel more closely bonded to your organization. These feelings of connection to the event and the organization may help plant the seeds for budding major donor relationships.

Create a life-long bond

It is not enough for an organization to have donors merely invest in their mission itself. Investments are done at arms length and may be impersonal. Organizations want donors to develop an emotional and life-long bond—to become part of their family. Similarly, organizations should want their galas to be more than just wonderful parties that people attend because they are fun and for a good cause. It is better if they become family celebrations and gatherings that represent keystone moments on a shared journey to accomplish a vital public interest objective.

Universities and many private high schools and other educational programs know this, as they have long focused on the life-long bond alumni relationships can create. These are celebrated and funds are raised around special class years during reunions. Reunion weekends have organically spawned tremendous innovation and creativity through their Web presence.

The reunion site

All the elements described for galas are regular features of many reunion Web sites. These sites are graphic intense with pictures of alumni, faculty, and students. These pages are also highly interactive, encouraging visitors to be involved through the site for a year or even more before the actual event. They serve, in this way, to build excitement. Any high school reunion today is likely to have some activity develop through commercial sites such as Classmates.com or similar resources. By the time the event happens, classmates have already connected and begun talking and sharing with one another.

A typical university reunion site will provide the schedule of events (why should anyone depend on the printed version which is so easily lost?). It will include a listing of the reunion committee members with e-mail addresses, so that everyone can provide input for the event early on. It will have a photo gallery, a full class list, and a variety of links to help graduates get caught up on information about the school today. It will have a section devoted to finding "lost" classmates who have moved away and for whom the event committee has no contact information.

Add a giving section

Of course, it will also have a giving section. These may describe special projects the class members have decided to join together to fund, or it could describe a variety of giving options. Reunion classes enjoy seeing how much they have raised, so a total to date is likely to be included. And just to further enhance the excitement of giving, there may be a friendly competition for the most dollars among different class years.

Many fundraisers feel that the purpose of special reunion fundraising efforts is to "bump up" giving over the alumni donor's lifetime. So while donors may give $25 each year their first few years out, perhaps by their 5th reunion, they will leap to $100 and may remain at about that level until their 10th or 25th, by which time they may leap to being $500 or $1,000 donors. In addition, reunions are a time when major gift giving becomes a special focus for fundraising. The Internet reunion site is designed to help bolster these efforts. If their popularity is any sign, then they are succeeding. Just one of many enjoyable examples can be found in the online press release of a recent $5 million class gift from Denison University's 50th reunion *(http://www.denison.edu/publicaffairs/pressreleases/reunion_2004.html).*

Sometimes reunion sites are predominantly managed by volunteers. The organization might give over some control over the design so that volunteers rather than staff can develop the site. This can be a good idea for any school or organization that is concerned with the staff time it might take to manage a reunion site.

One of the conveniences of a reunion Web site is the ability for participants to register and pay for their participation in the event. Online registering, however, is turning out to be much more than just a convenience. It's turning out to be a boon for fundraising.

Special events that require registration

Today's walk-a-thon, bike-a-thon, and similar public fundraising events are benefiting hugely from organized online registration and fundraising. These kinds of fundraising events succeed when they are heavily attended. While a gala has limited seating and reunions are limited only to alumni graduates, walks can become enormous events in which hundreds or thousands participate. The sheer number of participants helps achieve the media coverage and visibility sought and the giving, because it's smaller on average, benefits by larger and larger attendance totals.

In years past, a family that was dealing with a devastating illness might join in a walk-a-thon. In the weeks before the event, they would take gifts and pledges through their personal solicitation of friends and family. They would call, write, or visit the individuals they were asking. It takes a significant commitment of time to do this.

Organize teams online

Today, most major walks organize their teams online. Commercial resources make this relatively simple to do. Typically, a person connected to the organization signs up online to be a team captain. The site will automatically allow a high degree of personalization. The volunteer can add personal pictures, personalize the message, and set his or her personal goals.

The sites then automate much of the fundraising (see *personal fundraising pages* in Chapter 6). Just add the names and addresses of those you know (transcribe them all right from your e-mail address book) and decide if you want the pre-written solicitation or if you would like to make it your own. Your friends and family can click right from the e-mail message they get, give the gift by credit card (secured communications, of course), and then appear soon after on a scrolling banner of donors.

The volunteer's donors can return as needed to check on the progress toward the fundraising goal. They may even see the progress in a traditional fundraiser's "thermometer" and might decide to give a bit more to put the team over the top. The volunteer can get regular reports on progress. It's almost like giving them their own fundraising staff.

Generate financial support from nonparticipants

Many elements contribute to making this approach successful. It saves volunteers a lot of time, effort, and money, so they can be more active solicitors. Volunteer fundraisers can reach out to friends and family globally, yet personally. Because it is easier, it engages fundraising from those who may not be quite as focused or dedicated to the organization at this point. In the past, walk teams were comprised mostly of the diehard loyal donors and volunteers. Online fundraising broadens the participation. Many participants may not even attend the walk at all—but are happy to have helped raise the level of philanthropic support for something they do indeed care about.

> **Capital campaigns benefit from use of the Internet by providing—**
>
> - **a customized online home base for the campaign**
> - **the ability to communicate information and successes in real time**
> - **a marketing tool that can be targeted to a select population of donors**
> - **a nexus for institutional Web sites that may have been developed at different organization campuses without any coordination**

In addition, donors report that fundraising in this way is simply fun. For many, asking for annual support from friends and family is an excuse to contact them. They may personalize their message for each one in order to catch up. How many of us need that excuse to contact Uncle Jack or our best friend from high school? The beneficiaries of this are the nonprofit organizations who are gaining greater support and more awareness and visibility for themselves and their missions.

This kind of approach recently has caught fire in political fundraising. Popularized by Howard Dean's primary campaign for the Democratic Party's 2004 presidential nomination, online fundraising has become a mainstay in all major campaigns.

Again, Web sites automate a personalized fundraising campaign by individuals. They can do much the same work that walk fundraisers are doing online. A popular addition to these is encouraging such volunteer fundraisers to organize "house parties" or "meet ups" (see *http://www.meetup.com*) to bring like-minded individuals together to raise support. Unlike the walk efforts online, these events use the Internet to connect neighbors who do not know each other. Geographic proximity and a common interest in a candidate or cause is what connects the participants. They value finding one another and possibly staying connected socially. And they value supporting the cause for which they gathered.

Use automation and volunteers

In essence, this online fundraising technique is creating a mini-gala model, letting volunteers take over everything—providing a place for the event, food, invitations, and so on. All that the organization needs to do is to receive the check and use it wisely. Of course, to be very successful, the organization needs to support these efforts, providing the volunteers with good materials, both videos and printed, in order to make the event worthwhile for the participants. The most successful house party efforts may involve a phone-in period during which the candidate addresses multiple events simultaneously.

Innovative new and cutting-edge efforts such as these are in their early stages, but there are good signs that they represent how the Internet is creating a more diverse set of fundraising practices under the broad net of special events. They appeal particularly to a younger new generation of fundraising volunteer—individuals comfortable with utilizing technology to build grassroots efforts.

Many of these first generation efforts still have a rough feel to them. In the future, we will see them become more elegant and much more common, perhaps in other fundraising venues. How long will it be before we see a neighborhood food pantry or a church group using the Internet to support its fundraising in some of these ways and with some of these tools?

Make online fundraising event administration routine

We will also continue to see the Internet change special event fundraising in more dramatic ways. Organizations are already exploring the idea of using the Internet to actually be "at" a live event. Through video broadcasts over the Internet, it is now possible for individuals to attend seminars and hear speeches online. The Internet has become a common venue for certain fundraising events.

To sum up, the Internet's benefit for special events includes a number of very basic ideas, such as using a Web site to publicize and draw in more participants and even gifts before and after the event. It includes some important broader concepts, as well, such as employing the Internet to help build a different kind of connection to the organization, one that is more participatory and intimate while also more convenient.

Capital Campaigns

The capital campaign has become a way of life for many organizations, especially universities, public radio and television stations, and religious institutions. Not long ago, capital campaigns were held only occasionally and usually for a special need. Today, the planning for the next often begins as soon as the previous one ends.

Capital campaigns build public excitement around fundraising. They serve to identify a set of needs and priorities, and in so doing make an organization's strategic plans a little more accessible to the organization's donor constituency. Capital campaigns also help make larger solicitations easier, creating urgency and the motivation of achieving a goal.

As capital campaigns have become more popular, they have given birth to the campaign Web site. As suggested above, the primary goals of a campaign Web site are to present the fundraising priorities and to generate excitement around giving.

Typical campaign sites include many or all of the following features:

1. *A goal stated on the first page.* This can take the form of a graph or "thermometer" showing progress toward the goal. It will also include stories of key leadership gifts in the campaign.

2. *Messages from the campaign chair or others about the effort.* Often these are done in video or audio clips, as well as text, especially if high profile individuals or celebrities are helping to lead the campaign.

3. *A case statement in .pdf format.* The traditional case statement provides donors with a well-designed printed piece that explains the needs and attempts to motivate philanthropy toward them.

4. *Detailed information about the institution.* Even institutions with complete Web sites will often reorganize and re-present their factual data, organizational structure, and history. Many campaign Web sites have a completely separate look from the main Web site of the organization. The purposes of doing this are to deliberately contrast with what the donors are used to on the site and thus grab their attention, or to create a more polished and prestigious look to appeal to high-scale donors. An organization with an extremely well branded look may simply want to draw greater attention by adopting a new campaign logo with different color schemes and page designs. The University of Chicago did this with its campaign website at *http:// chicagoinitiative.uchicago.edu/*. Here even the URL is unique. You can see the logo and color scheme versus the university's home page at: *http:// www.uchicago.edu*. If the capital campaign is sufficiently large, then sub-branding or branding differently may be a good strategy. It may not be worth doing for smaller campaigns.

5. *A list of needs and complete detail on them, as well as recognition levels.* These may be replicated in the case statement, but don't count on everyone printing out that document.

6. *Pictures.* Appropriate pictures here are of people, program beneficiaries, and model construction planned. Some will include video feeds, allowing visitors to monitor 24 hours/day building projects under construction.

7. *Current news.* News stories may help ensure that the site looks lively and up-to-date. The campaign Web site can be viewed as a secondary portal into the organization.

Market to donors rather than to the public

In essence, capital campaign Web sites recast the organization's online presence and market the organization very specifically to donors rather than the public at large. While the main gateway to the organization typically is focused on its mission, with philanthropy carefully and appropriately woven in, the campaign Web site can be unabashed in its drive for dollars. In a role reversal, fundraising becomes the highest priority on these pages, and the mission is woven in to show how essential fundraising is to meeting the organization's objectives.

Capital campaigns also often take place at large complex institutions and can serve an ancillary role of unifying multiple fundraising efforts. In a university, they bring together all of the college, graduate, and professional schools toward a common goal. They may connect geographically separate campuses, or organizations with separate chapters. The new Web portal can be a place to reflect that unity and to demonstrate the interconnectedness of an organization with multiple parts.

Resources

American Cancer Society

http://www.cancer.org/docroot/home/index.asp

Visit the Mosaic of Memories pages *(http://www.cancer.org/docroot/DON/DON_2_Mosaic_of_Memories.asp)* for information about creating online tributes to loved ones. When we last looked at the beginning of 2006, almost 150 donors had set up these Web pages. Each page has a picture of the person being honored, a link to submit a testimonial, a link to read the testimonials of others, and a link to submit a donation in honor of the deceased.

American Civil Liberties Union

http://www.aclu.org/

Start by clicking on the "donate now" button on the home page for options on how to join or donate. You can find planned giving, monthly giving plans, online and offline giving, and all kinds of ways to support the organization in a user-friendly format.

American Heart Association (General Fundraising)
http://www.americanheart.org/presenter.jhtml?identifier=1200018

Here you can find e-cards, workplace giving, planned giving, details about the "Dear Neighbor" campaign (folks recruited to send fundraising solicitation letters to their neighbors), and special events.

American Red Cross

http://www.redcross.org

The American Red Cross has developed an exemplary Web site that facilitates donations of cash, products, airline miles, and blood and body organs and tissues. It is colorful, well-organized, and its museum gift shop sells useful products such as emergency kits and logo-laden clothing. For examples of pages to imitate, see the donor recognition pages *(http://www.redcrosslegacy.org/donor.php)*, its planned giving pages *(http://www.redcrosslegacy.org/* and *http://www.redcross.org/general/ 0,1082,0_212_,00.html)*, and in-kind giving information *(http://www.redcross.org/donate/goods/)*.

Ask.com
http://www.ask.com

Ask.com (formerly "Ask Jeeves") is a search engine that uses common English questions that the user types in rather than the esoteric Boolean search terms required by many of its competitors. It is also a search engine of search engines. Type in a question such as "Where can I find information about e-philanthropy?" or simply type in "e-philanthropy," and its search spider will return some of the most likely matches you are looking for from a handful of popular search engines, such as Web Crawler and Alta Vista. Using this site may save time if you would otherwise be performing searches on more than one search engine.

Cyclura
http://www.cyclura.com/modules.php?op=modload&name=News&file=article&sid=137

This is a nice donor recognition page of an organization whose mission is to support conservation groups and organizations of endangered species and promotes awareness of lizards.

David Lamb's Prospect Research Page
http://www.lambresearch.com/

The links here are organized into ten categories, such as directories, public records, and reference.

Dogpile
http://www.dogpile.com

Dogpile is a search engine and directory that performs metasearches of other search engines when you activate its "metasearch" function. Type in your keywords, and the engine will find matches in at least 10 other popular search engines.

Edgar Online People
http://access.edgar-online.com/people/peopleSearch.asp

This site, much of it free, will give you leads into the business affiliations of prospects. EDGAR contains only the affiliations of individuals who are associated with publicly-held companies in the capacity of either insider, director, or 5% owner. Since there are around 14,000 publicly-held companies versus around 18 million private companies, most prospects will not be found here.

Forbes.com
http://www.forbes.com/

If your prospect is well-heeled and in business, this searchable site will unearth nuggets that you might not even find on a search engine as comprehensive as Google.

Google
http://www.google.com

The Google search engine has access to more than 8 billion unique Web pages and more than a billion images, and is becoming the standard first place to start when researching a potential donor. Click on the "Jobs, Press & Help" menu on the home page for useful tips on making your search efficient and effective.

Habitat for Humanity International
https://www.habitat.org/giving/donate.aspx?link=1

This page has a form to donate securely online, as well as an adjacent box that tells you what your donation can provide (e.g., $150 for a front door). The home page at *http://www.habitat.org/default2.aspx* prominently features links to the donation and online store pages, and links to pages for tribute gifts and monthly giving. Participating monthly givers receive an online newsletter.

Hoover's Online
http://hoovweb.hoovers.com/free/

While Hoover's is the Rolls Royce of prospect researcher sites, the service charges a substantial subscription fee. Some services continue to be free, however, and it's worth a look. Start your search by clicking on "executive's name" and go from there.

Internet Prospector
http://www.internet-prospector.org/

This non-commercial site has a free electronic newsletter. It is staffed by "a network of volunteers who mine the Net for prospect research nuggets." Visit the "reference desk" for links organized by topics, such as "corporations" and "people."

Lycos
http://www.lycos.com

Lycos is a directory, search engine, and online community. "Add Your Site to Lycos" can be found at the bottom left of the home page. A search on the term "e-philanthropy" yielded two hits based on user traffic and 224 Web sites that had the term in a search of the complete Lycos catalog.

Melissa Data Corporation Lookups
http://www.melissadata.com/Lookups/index.htm

By clicking on the "Campaign Contributions" menu, you can search by ZIP Code for individuals who contributed at least $200 to a federal election campaign for each of several election cycles. There are other databases available on this site with prospect research applications, but when we pointed out this site at a workshop conducted at a state conference of the Association of Fundraising Professionals, everyone was simply blown away by the utility of this particular free resource.

Mercyhurst College (Capital Campaign)
http://www.mercyhurst.edu/giving/capital-campaign.php

This is a good example of a capital giving site. It must have been quite effective as, when we reviewed the site, fundraising goals for both the 75th anniversary campaign and the Alden science challenge had been exceeded.

MSU Library's Prospect Research Resources
http://www.lib.msu.edu/harris23/grants/prospect.htm

After performing your routine Google search on a prospect, this is perhaps the next best place to visit—but make sure you call home first and say you might be working late, as you might not want to come up for air for awhile.

The Nature Conservancy (Planned Giving)
http://www.nature.org/joinanddonate/giftandlegacy/

We found this to be one of the better, more comprehensive planned giving sites.

NETSource @ USC
http://www.usc.edu/dept/source/

You can find links to lots of free and low-cost databases here. We particularly found the links to salary information interesting *(see http://www.usc.edu/dept/source/Salary.htm)*.

Sanilac District Library
http://www.sanilacdistrictlibrary.lib.mi.us/g-recognition.html

This is an example of a virtual donor plaque. See a screen shot of this page on page 160.

Special Olympics Wisconsin (Major Gifts)
http://www.specialolympicswisconsin.org/ways_to_give_campaign.html

The major gifts department at this organization has its own pages, with donor recognition being a prominent part of them. It has a nice feel to it, combining stories of those served by the organization with photos, information about fundraising events, planned giving pages, and links to organization sponsors.

Yahoo!
http://www.yahoo.com

Yahoo! (which is an acronym for "You always have other options") is a directory, search engine, and online community. If you only register with one directory, this would be our choice. Yahoo!'s main directory is enormous and well organized—an important combination for the Internet— resulting in a valuable and easy-to-access way to find what you need.

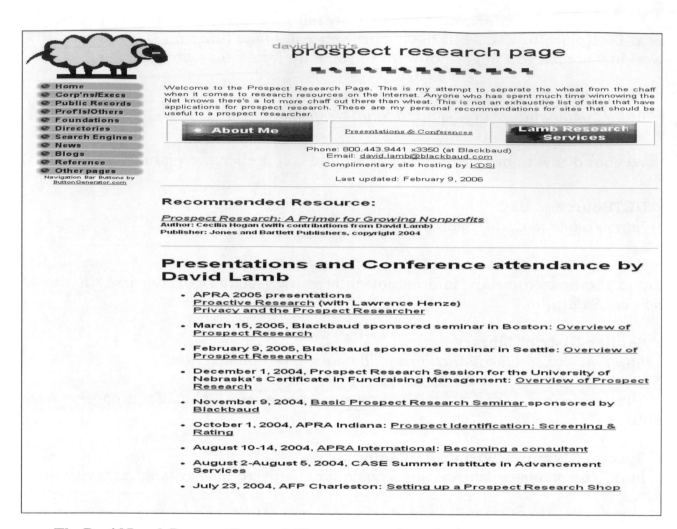

The David Lamb Prospect Research Home page at: http://www.lambresearch.com. Reprinted with permission.

Chapter 4

Using E-mail, Electronic Newsletters, and Podcasts to Communicate Organizational Needs to Stakeholders

E-mail is still considered the "killer application" of the Internet, and with good reason. For charities that abuse it, it may well, indeed, earn its name. A charity that purchases a disk with 20 million e-mail names on it and then indiscriminately e-mails a fundraising solicitation to the list is *likely* to make a name for itself. That name will be spelled "M-U-D." There is a consensus that using such a strategy is about as injudicious as one can get in using e-mail for fundraising. Our culture accepts the "cost" of wading through junk snail mail, most of it from tax-exempt organizations seeking contributions. Perhaps there is a feeling that the sender at least made some effort to weed out duplicates and, at least, is trying to target the mailing because even the charitable bulk mail postage rate is getting fairly steep these days. Printing fundraising letters, return envelopes, and the "free gift inside" of personalized mailing labels, calendars, or greeting cards must cost something, let alone the cost of designing and sending out the mailing.

Avoiding Spamming

We do not (and should not!) as yet feel the same way about unsolicited e-mail. Pornographers, scam artists, crooks "phishing" for personal financial information, and purveyors of illegal drugs send a high percentage of the "spam" mail we all receive. Sending "spam" mail may associate an organization with these types of unsavory operations. No organization should want that.

The culture of participation in the Internet community is still evolving. What is not totally clear is what types of e-mail solicitation are acceptable, and what types are the most effective. Communicating organizational needs by e-mail to stakeholders who already have some relationship with the organization, such as donors, board members, and those served by the organization, is usually appropriate. Sending out online newsletters to an organization's stakeholders who have opted in to receive them is even better.

> **Online fundraisers must recognize—**
>
> - **spamming donors and potential donors is forbidden**
> - **the opt-in electronic newsletter is becoming the online fundraising and friendraising medium of choice**
> - **charities need to develop a strategy to collect e-mail addresses from their stakeholders and supporters**
> - **getting friends and supporters to send e-mails on behalf of the organization is an effective strategy compared to direct e-mailing**

Using E-mail to Interact With Stakeholders

One legitimate use of direct e-mail is to simply interact with your stakeholders and provide them with information and services that bring them closer to your organization. E-mail is a cost-effective means for increasing direct communication between your organization's actual and potential donors. Because of the convenience of the "reply" button available within all e-mail programs, it also provides a convenient way for getting feedback. Sharing timely and informative news about what your organization is doing, and plans to do in the future, can keep your organization on the minds of your donors and maintain your visibility. Among information that can be shared with broadcast e-mails are the following:

- new features added to the organization's Web site
- requests for volunteers to help the organization with a program or service
- calls to action, such as to send letters or e-mails to public officials concerning an important, emerging public policy issue

- directions on how to participate in an online or offline survey
- information about an upcoming fundraiser
- details about an upcoming meeting or program (with driving directions)

Of course, even those who have expressed interest in your organization in the past may no longer maintain that enthusiasm. We recommend that you place instructions at the bottom of any mass-distributed e-mail on how to be deleted from the list for future e-mails.

Collecting E-Mail Addresses

Almost universally, online fundraising advocates agree that seeking a donor's e-mail address is a positive strategy, even if there are no current plans to communicate with those donors online. Plans can change. E-mail remains the fastest and cheapest way an organization can communicate, even if it may not be the most appropriate way in every circumstance. But simply having the capacity to contact every stakeholder quickly by e-mail is considered to be a top objective by those of us who give advice about online fundraising.

There are obvious strategies that will increase the percentage of donors who will give your organization their e-mail addresses. Organizations should routinely include "e-mail address" as a field in their donation forms and other forms (such as those used to request additional information from the organization). The online newsletter subscription is also a good method used to harvest e-mail addresses from donors and supporters. Some organizations require Web visitors to register with their e-mail addresses and other identifying information if they want to have access to some features of the site, such as the online community.

E-Mail Appending

A more costly approach is to use a commercial service called "e-mail appending." This involves providing the names of donors to a business that has a large database of e-mail addresses. For a fee, typically 25 cents per match, the business will provide you with an e-mail address that matches to a street address from your donor database. The matches can be provided without any prescreening by the company (not recommended), so that the organization simply has the e-mail addresses that match. The downside of this is that the organization's donors may not be delighted that their e-mail address has fallen into the hands of the organization. A second way to obtain these addresses is for the service to determine if the donor is willing to permit his or her e-mail address to be shared with the charity ("opt-in") and provide e-mail addresses to the charity ONLY from those donors who have given their permission. A third way is for the service to e-mail the donors and indicate that their e-mail addresses will be forwarded to the charity unless the donor sends an e-mail requesting that this not be done ("opt-out").

As we write this, there is a continuing debate as to whether e-mail appending is a legitimate way for a charity to obtain the e-mail addresses of its donors. First, there is skepticism about the trustworthiness of the third party providers. Executives of charities anecdotally are reporting problems with the accuracy of the matches and whether the e-mail addresses they receive have truly been screened as they request, as either opt-in or opt-out.

It is clearly much cheaper and less obtrusive for a charity to obtain a donor's e-mail address directly when the donation is made, whether this donation is made online or offline. We recommend that charities not miss any opportunity to obtain the e-mail address directly from donors, under conditions in which the donor is offering informed consent.

Turn your web site into a catcher's mitt

The organization's Web site offers lots of opportunities to obtain these e-mail addresses, such as through electronic newsletter subscriptions, online surveys, information requests, e-mail feedback to the organization, and similar online transactions in which the e-mail address is routinely needed to respond. As Mathew Emery, of the application service provider Kintera, explained at a 2004 workshop on e-philanthropy sponsored by the Pennsylvania Association of Nonprofit Organizations, "The Web site has been (typically) treated like it's a brochure, but it's really a catcher's mitt. You want something on every single page where you can find something about the visitor." According to Emery, even if a donor doesn't make an online donation, online communications have a positive effect on direct mail. His organization found that there was a 10% increase in donations made as a result of a direct mail fundraising piece when an e-mail was sent to donors prior to sending out the direct mail.

E-Mail to a Friend Strategies

Another fundraising strategy that appears to be effective is the online version of getting organization supporters to write personal letters to those they know, including friends and neighbors, appealing for donations. In the offline version, a charity might make a call to a past donor. Rather than requesting a direct donation, the charity requests that the donor send a note to ten or twenty neighbors requesting a donation. If the donor agrees, the charity provides the names of those it desires to solicit, perhaps a sample letter, and if appropriate, other support.

In the online version of this technique, donors are asked to e-mail their friends and relatives with a donor appeal. The solicitations are not considered spam, because they are coming from personal friends and relatives. Recipients of the solicitations see the communication coming from someone they know, rather than an organization, and are more likely to open the e-mail and respond.

There is increasing evidence that this type of e-mail solicitation is effective. One application service provider, Kintera, has developed software to facilitate such online volunteer fundraising, called "Friends Asking Friends®." Kintera reports that its 3,352 campaigns utilizing this software raised $192 million in the 12 months ending in March 2004, $48 million of which was donated online. This approach is particularly effective for specific fundraising events, in which an organization's supporters e-mail their online contacts about an upcoming charity auction, race/walk, or benefit concert. The Kintera software package has integrated links providing information and the ability to donate or register for the event, and tracks donations and responses (see *Personal Fundraising Pages* in Chapter 6).

Electronic Newsletters

An electronic newsletter, sent by e-mail to those who have voluntarily requested to become subscribers, is becoming the model of choice for fundraising and friendraising. Unlike indiscriminately sent direct e-mail, this model of indirect fundraising appears to be both ethical and effective, and is considered a useful service by recipients. The electronic newsletter is a periodic e-mail that includes content that would be appropriate for an organization's print newsletter. The advantages are that compared to a print newsletter, there are no printing costs, no postage costs, no labels to be printed out and affixed, and minimal time-lag between the time the material is written and the time it goes to "press." Direct and indirect fundraising solicitations can be embedded within the newsletter, along with advocacy alerts, information about organization successes, upcoming fundraising events, calls for volunteers, notices concerning fee-based services, details about new laws and regulations that affect the organization's constituency, information about new Web sites of interest to stakeholders, jobs that may be available within your organization or similar ones, new features of the organization's Web site, and so on.

Some organizations solicit advertising for their electronic newsletters, or embed simple links or a clickable link logo of a business partner who has agreed to pay a sponsor fee.

Unlike telephone and direct mail, an e-mail newsletter comes with little or no price tag other than staff time. It provides a valuable service to your donors and friends, and many look forward to receiving these regular communications in their in-box. We can't think of any downside to it. Typically, your organization's Web site will have a simple form that permits viewers to enter their e-mail address to subscribe to the newsletter.

It is technically possible to maintain your electronic newsletter using your e-mail software. But doing so is cumbersome at best, and it uses up the available bandwidth your Internet Service Provider (ISP) permits. Many ISPs impose limits on the number of e-mails that can be sent with the identical message.

Consider third parties to administer electronic mail lists

Fortunately, free and low cost software packages (such as Dada Mail) are available on the Web that permit administration of electronic mailing lists. Many Web site hosts will permit you to send out thousands of e-mails to those who have opted in to receive them. If your host limits your use of e-mail, there are for-profit providers that will send your newsletter out for you using their own servers. In the event that you do not wish to tie up your own Web server, these third party services may be a good investment.

Here is some advice for planning your electronic newsletter:

- Provide the newsletter only to those who opt in by taking a positive step to subscribe, such as clicking on a button on your Web site. Sending out these e-mails to those who have not opted in is considered spam. At best, it is annoying. At worst, it could result in your ISP taking away your service, as well as infuriating your donors and other stakeholders.

- Advertise the availability of the newsletter on all organization materials.

- Make sure the electronic newsletter provides value to the readership, so subscribers won't automatically delete it or unsubscribe.

- Provide information in each newsletter on how to unsubscribe, preferably with a link to do so, and honor each unsubscribe request.

- Don't sell, rent, or give away your list of e-mail addresses.

- While it is acceptable to include advertising in your newsletter, use it sparingly. If you are using a third-party mailing list service, be willing to pay a few dollars more to purchase the "premium" version rather than using the free version that includes advertising solicited by the application service provider. Some of the ads accepted by the application service provider may be considered inappropriate by your readership and reflect poorly on your organization.

- Provide an opportunity for subscribers to donate to your organization if they choose to, such as by providing a link to your Web site's donation form, publicizing a specific "wish list" of items that could be donated or financed, and including information about planned giving opportunities.

Some issues to consider when choosing whether to administer your mailing list on your ISP's or Web host's server or through an application service provider are:

- *The amount of bandwidth required.* If your newsletter is simple text and is sent out to only a few subscribers, your requirements will be less than if your newsletter contains high-resolution pictures in an HTML format and is sent to tens of thousands.

- *Constraints of your application service provider.* You may be unable to send out your newsletter using your current Web host because of technical limitations.

- *How your subscribers will subscribe and unsubscribe.* This can be opt-in, opt-out, or even better, double opt-in, which means that subscribers who have hit the subscribe button receive an e-mail asking them to confirm that they want to subscribe before their e-mail address is entered into the subscriber database.

- *How bounced messages will be handled.* This includes addresses from those whose e-mail inbox is full or who no longer have an active e-mail address.

- *How you will deal with advertising.* Advertising, if you will permit it, can be solicited by your own organization, or inserted by an application service provider in exchange for the use of free newsletter administration software.

- *Who on the staff will be responsible for newsletter content and mailing list management.* There is work involved in creating the newsletter, soliciting advertisements and sponsorships, and dealing with bounced addresses.

HTML-formatted e-mail and newsletters

Most people despise spam e-mails. But we sometimes are impressed by the design of some of these, utilizing slick fonts, graphics, backgrounds, pictures, and catchy special effects. While there are advantages in keeping an electronic newsletter simple by keeping it text-only, an eye-catching electronic newsletter can have the same appeal as a well-designed print newsletter. Sending your newsletter in HTML format also provides you with the option of personalizing the messages, not only in the header, but in the body of the message, as well.

Standard e-mail programs such as Outlook and Eudora permit limited formatting, such as using different typefaces, font sizes, bold, italics, and indenting. More sophisticated software, such as Dreamweaver, permits you to insert backgrounds, tables, and graphics. Another option is to use software that is specifically designed for sending out bulk HTML-formatted e-mail. Among the more reasonably priced programs are Enewsletter Manager, Group Mail, and World Merge. If you still feel clueless, you can simply hire an application service provider with experience in setting up HTML e-mails—there are scores of them.

There are some technical issues to resolve if you do decide to send out HTML-based newsletters and e-mail. First, what you send will look different depending on the browser being used to view it. Some recipients may not be able to see it at all, depending on their e-mail program. You need to pre-test it using all of the most popular viewers, such as Outlook, AOL, and Hotmail. For more practical advice, you can visit the Techsoup Web site *(http://www.techsoup.org)* for articles about electronic newsletters and e-mail.

Podcasts

As we write this, the podcast craze is now sweeping the nation. It is adding another arrow in the quiver for charities that want to send a targeted audio or video message to stakeholders in a timely, convenient, and most importantly, cost-effective way.

Back in the 1980s and 1990s when Gary Grobman was the CEO of a statewide association, he would get occasional requests to appear on a "live on tape" radio or TV show to discuss public policy issues that his organization was dealing with. He would dutifully spend precious time preparing to be interviewed, drive to the station, and wait what seemed like hours for the interview to start. Almost without fail, the shows would broadcast at a time when it was quite unlikely that anyone would ever listen to what he had to say. It was rare that he ever heard from anyone who had actually listened to the program he was on.

Podcasting changes all of this. It makes *you* the producer of a radio show (or TV show), and gives you the ability to reach your target audience when they are most perceptive to hearing what you want to say about your charity.

Examples of podcasting by nonprofit organizations

The Royal Society for the Protection of Birds, a UK-based charity founded in 1889, podcasts regularly with the sounds of birds and other wildlife. To hear an example, point your browser to: *http://www.rspb.org.uk/england/central/cons_action/ podcast.asp*

Reverend Nancy McDonald Ladd of the Bull Run Unitarian Universalists in Manassas, Virginia, offers her weekly sermons by podcast, attracting an audience of members who live too far away to conveniently attend services, and the congregants' children who are away at college. And a growing segment of the audience appears to be those who attend the Sunday service and want to hear the sermon again when it becomes available by RSS (Really Simple Syndication, the protocol that supports subscriptions of podcast and blog broadcasts) feed on Tuesday. According to national church leaders, Bull Run is just one of 25 Unitarian churches around the nation that podcast all or some of their weekly services.

The Collective Heritage Institute, also known as "Bioneers," is a nonprofit organization that promotes practical environmental solutions and innovative social strategies for restoring the Earth and communities. If you point your Web browser to *http://www.podcast.net,* you can find a directory of Bioneer's podcasts of ten shows the nonprofit organization produced for public radio during the previous six months. You can hear them with the click of a mouse—a lot simpler than waiting for a radio broadcast.

On December 1, 2005, the Campaign to Make Poverty History joined with Gcast.com to launch the first ONE podcast. The World AIDS Day ONEcast featured former President of South Africa Nelson Mandela, Bono, U2 lead singer and co-founder of DATA (Debt, AIDS, Trade for Africa), and Chris Martin of Coldplay, along with members of the faith community and other ONE supporters. That month, Bono's charity ONE: The Campaign To Make Poverty History launched a monthly podcast focusing on AIDS, hunger in Africa, and other social issues.

What is podcasting?

Podcasting refers to the creation of audio files that you can upload to the Internet, using a process that enables the subscriber of the broadcast to receive information that this audio program is available to be downloaded to the subscriber's audio player or computer. These files are typically in MP3 format and 5 to 60 minutes in duration, making them suitable for hearing on the subscriber's computer or personal audio player, such as an iPOD or other MP3 player.

Advantages and disadvantages

What makes podcasting an incredibly powerful means of communication is that anyone in the world with an Internet connection can listen to podcasts at any time he or she chooses. This contrasts to cable TV and radio shows, which are on at a specific time and require action on the part of the viewer/listener to first know that there is a program of interest and then take steps to either listen to it in real time or record it. With podcasting, the subscriber is in complete control using the technology, deciding what content to subscribe to, and when to hear it. Podcasting affords the capability of listening to the program over and over again, having the ability to store it indefinitely, rewinding it, pausing it, deleting it, transferring the program to other media such as a CD-ROM, and distributing the files freely to others. Usually, there is no advertising to listen to, although there is no law against a charity making a subtle plea for donations to support its mission.

To hear your program, all subscribers need is a media player, preferably portable, and an Internet connection. The broadcaster's costs for equipment are negligible, and the subscriber pays nothing for the service. Even if subscribers don't have an iPOD or equivalent, the broadcaster's Web site can be designed to permit listeners to click on a button and listen while they sit in front of the computer screen, with the capacity to download the file for future use.

How to podcast

The basic equipment needed to create a podcast consists of a microphone that connects to your computer, headphones, a computer, and an Internet connection. You can find detailed instructions on how to set up a podcast at sites such as Webmonkey *http://www.hotwired.com/webmonkey/* (search on the term "podcast") and Podcast411 *(http://www.podcast411.com/howto_1.html)*. The basic steps required are:

1. *Create your content.* This is accomplished by speaking into a microphone connected to your computer. The content can be whatever you might include if the organization were producing its own radio show: highlights of the organization's accomplishments, pending public policy issues and advocacy efforts that listeners can participate in, details about a new general fundraising or capital campaign, new programs and services offered by the organization, or new features of the organization's Web site. Software can easily blend in music (make sure you have permission to use it) to open and close the program. Record directly into the computer using programs such as Audacity for Windows/Mac or GarageBand for Mac. While it is not required, a good quality microphone and a room in which the sound isn't bouncing off the walls are of benefit.

2. *Use software to save your content as MP3 files.* Among such software titles that are available for downloading are RiverPast Audio Converter for Windows ($29.95 at *http://www.popularshareware.com/vc-rate.html)* and a free version of Audio Hijack for MAC *(http://www.rogueamoeba.com/audiohijack/download.php)*.

3. *Use software to edit your files.* Among popular software titles for this purpose are *Audacity (http://www.topdrawerdownloads.com/ showdownload.php?company=Audacity&title=Audacity);* GarageBand *(http://www.apple.com/ilife/garageband/),* Adobe Audition *(http:// www.download.com/Adobe-Audition/3000-2170_4-10324430.html),* and SoundStudio *(http://www.freeverse.com/soundstudio/).*

4. *Publish your podcast.* You have a choice of publishing it on your Web site or a site that serves as a catalog of podcasts (or both). Among the popular ones are:

OurMedia.org *(http://www.ourmedia.org)*
Itunes Music Store *(http://www.itunes.com/podcasts)*
IPodder *(http://www.ipodder.org)*
Podcast Alley *(http://www.podcastalley.com/)*
Podcasting News *(http://www.podcastingnews.com/)*
Podcast.net *(http://www.podcast.net)*

Why podcasting is the future

We remember a few decades ago when personal stereo headphones such as the Walkman became popular. Today, if you see someone walking down the street without talking into a cell phone, he or she is likely to have an earpiece connected to one of the 14 million iPODs sold by Apple in the last quarter of 2005 alone. And this doesn't count the millions of iPOD clones with the capability of downloading and storing MP3 files. In a massive shift in popular culture, demand responsiveness is how people want their information, and podcasting fits this perfectly.

For charities, podcasting is a natural fit, providing a forum to reach major givers with "insider" briefings about the organization, updates about programs funded by donations, details about a capital campaign, and opportunities to advocate on behalf of a public policy issue of importance to the organization.

Resources

CompanyNewsletters.com
http://www.companynewsletters.com/electronic.htm

Here you can find a useful article by David Kander, *How to Know What Kind of Online Newsletter to Publish.*

Dada Mail
http://mojo.skazat.com

Dada Mail is a popular free (open source) feature-rich e-mail management system that can be downloaded at this site.

Echoditto
http://www.echoditto.com/best/fundraising

This "Best Practices and Tips for Sending Email and Fundraising Online" advice column has plenty of good tips on what to put in your e-mail fundraising solicitation.

Ezine Manager
http://www.ezinemanager.com

This is the service used by Dr. Phil, according to the site. It is a free service if you send less than 250 e-mails each month. Otherwise expect to pay approximately $19.50 per month for sending up to 19,500 e-mails, with discounts for greater quantities.

GetActive.com
http://www.getactive.com/news_events/ga_today.html

Read articles about how to use e-mail effectively in your fundraising campaigns. Of particular value are links to articles on this page by Michael Stein, Brent Blackaby, Robert Weiner, and Madeline Stanionis.

The Gilbert E-mail Manifesto
http://news.gilbert.org/features/featureReader$3608

This essay about the importance of e-mail to fundraising, written by influential nonprofit organization Web guru Michael Gilbert, raised quite a stir when it was first published in 2001. Five years later, it provides what appears to be timeless advice for organizations obsessing over spending more resources on glitzy Web sites at the expense of e-mail campaigns.

Podcast411
http://www.podcast411.com

This site is entirely devoted to podcasting, including tutorials, directories, software, and news. The site also accesses Podscope, the first search engine that allows you to search for spoken words within any audio or video file. The site's management says it is starting with podcasts and will be adding all types of multimedia "in coming months." A search on the term "nonprofit" in January 2006 returned eight "hits" with links to hear the podcasts.

Ralph Wilson's *How to Develop an E-Mail Newsletter*
http://www.wilsonweb.com/articles/newsletter.htm

This classic article from a June 1998 issue of *Web Marketing Today* clearly explains why you should be offering an electronic newsletter on your site and the benefits of collecting e-mail addresses from your stakeholders.

Webmonkey
http://www.hotwired.com/webmonkey/

Search on the term "podcast" for detailed instructions on how to set up a Podcast.

Your Mailing List Provider
http://www.ymlp.com

Free mailing list management is available here for up to 1,000 subscribers if you are willing to accept the site's advertising. For the advertising-free version, expect to pay $2.50-$15 per month, depending on e-mail volume, for up to 10,000 monthly subscribers. A demo of the software can be found on the site.

The Gratz College Donations page at: http://www.gratz.edu/default.aspx?p=3969. Reprinted with permission.

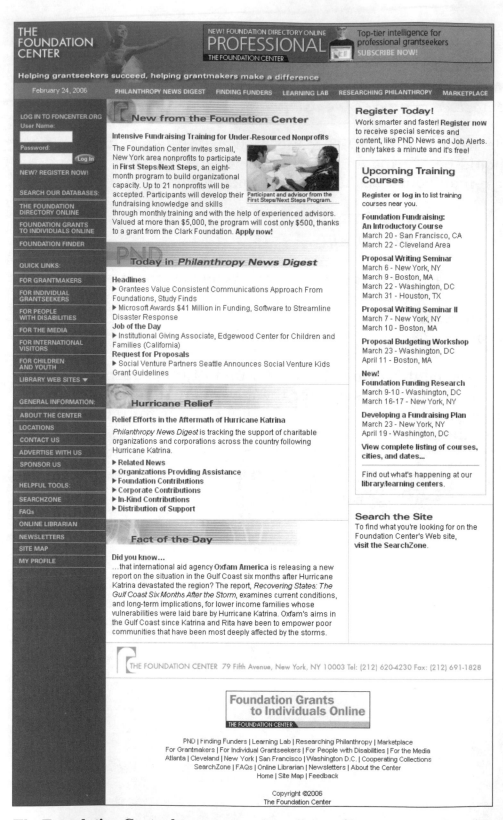

The Foundation Center home page at:http://www.fdncenter.org. Reprinted with permission. See a review of this Web site on page 20.

Chapter 5

Finding Grants on the Web

Searching for Funding Sources Online

Government agencies at all levels, foundations, and corporations have billions of dollars to give away each year to support the missions of worthy charitable organizations. Some of these grants come with substantial strings attached, and others can be used for almost any reasonable purpose. What they have in common is that information about these funding sources is usually posted on the Web sites of the funders, in addition to being available in databases that are often searchable by categories that will help you target your search.

It wasn't too long ago that nonprofit organizations were comfortable with budgeting thousands of dollars for thick directories of these funding opportunities. Now, many of these directories are available for a reasonable fee on CD-ROM, by subscription on the Internet, or for free at scores of Web sites. If you are looking for funding from such grantors, you need to know about these sites, which will save you countless hours of search for the funds you need.

Of the almost quarter-trillion dollars raised annually by charities, perhaps only 15% or so comes from sources other than individual donors, such as foundations run by individuals, families and corporations, community foundations, and corporate giving programs. Yet, there remains a certain caché to having a grant come from a prestigious foundation, providing your organization with instant credibility. The Internet has made it much easier to identify potential funders, using online directories and databases that are searchable by the funder's program priorities, geography, and type of support. Today, almost all major foundations have a Web site, as do many of the smaller ones. Among typical documents posted are mission and values statements, annual reports, newsletters, grant opportunities, biographies of staff and leadership, funding priorities, guidelines and deadlines, information about previous grants made (including amounts of funding awarded), and, to an increasing degree, application forms that can be submitted electronically.

Identify most likely funding sources

The first objective in a search for funding sources is identifying potential grantmakers that have a history of awarding grants in your charity's area of interest in your geographical area. Among the obvious targets are—

- private foundations—non-governmental organizations with an endowment derived principally from a single source (individual, family, or corporation) that makes grants for charitable purposes
- corporate giving programs—grant-making programs within a for-profit business
- public foundations—charities that make grants to unrelated organizations and individuals
- community foundations—charities that make grants to organizations within a specific locality or region
- government—federal, state, regional, and local governments

Identify foundation funding

Many nonprofit organizations depend on foundation support to maintain their programs. But with all the progress offered by the Internet, foundations will not come to your site to give. Despite that, grant writers were among the first to benefit from the access the Internet provided them to look for and approach foundations whose objectives match their missions and to manage the process of applying for grants.

Through the Foundation Center's Web site *(http://www.fdncenter.org)*, grantseekers can find a particular foundation or research those most likely to be attracted to their programs by areas of interest, type of funding, or the geographical region they support. The Foundation Directory, long a vital resource for fundraisers, is available online here.

- **Government, foundations, and corporations are all sources of funding that can be found on the Internet**
- **It is important to research the grantor before applying for funds**
- **There are free Web-based, searchable databases that assist in finding funders**
- **In-kind donations from corporations are an increasing resource for charities**

White Hat Communications

Fundraisers can read a foundation's guidelines on its Web site and learn how to apply. Many allow proposals to be sent online or by e-mail. The Internet provides a convenient way to ensure that you are sending the best possible proposal, and it helps foundation staff, as they have to answer fewer questions. Fundraisers should always consult a foundation's Web site before contacting a program officer with questions. It is wise to become intimately familiar with a foundation by reading through its site before and during the process of applying.

Foundation staff frequently complain when charities call with questions that were clearly answered on their Web site. Demonstrate to them the courtesy of looking there first. At the same time, while it has become increasingly possible to find a grant and apply for it entirely online, we caution against this. Make "personal" contact with the grantmaker before applying. Tell the staff if you found useful information at the site. We recommend that this be done by telephone or letter. However, follow-up e-mail requests for information or responses to questions are perfectly acceptable.

> **Fundraisers can use the Internet to—**
>
> - **identify foundations that support the organization's mission**
> - **find information about the foundations and those who make funding decisions**
> - **use online databases to find appropriate foundation support**

Some of the information you can find at a foundation's Web site includes announcements about grants the funder has already made, contact information, strategic plans, annual reports, and other documents you will find useful in crafting your proposal. You can often find useful information from the grantmaker's federal tax return (usually a 990 or 990PF) at such sites as Guidestar *(http://www.guidestar.org)* or GrantSmart *(http://www.grantsmart.org)*. The searchable GrantSmart database has more than 300,000 federal tax returns from more than 85,000 private foundations and charitable trusts. You can also use popular search engines such as Google *(http://www.google.com)* to find general information about the grantmaker, those that have received funding from it, and the grantmaker staff.

Thank and acknowledge support

Cultivate a strong relationship by publicly acknowledging foundation support on your organization's site. Do this in much the same way as you might your individual donors, through donor listings, or even a dedicated page or online press release announcing the gift and describing the foundation's history and matching objectives. If you have done this, be sure to let the foundation know how you have acknowledged its support.

Access free and low-cost databases

Want to search community foundations by state? Point your browser to: *http://www.tgci.com/funding/community.asp* to tap into the Grantsmanship Center's database. You can find grant sources organized by topic (e.g., children and youth, recreation, arts & cultural activities, and the aged) at *http://www.Lib.msu.edu/harris23/grants/2sgalpha.htm.*

• Visit the Foundation Center *(http://www.fdncenter.org*—see "finding funders") for searchable databases that help identify potential funding sources. Here you can find basic information about 73,000 private and community foundations, including their assets, amount of grants, contact information, and Web site address. By the end of 2005, this site had links to more than 4,800 Web sites of foundations. This site also has links to the annual federal tax returns of many of these organizations. One useful feature is the "SEARCHZONE" available from the home page. Here you can type in a keyword and find matches from descriptions of these foundations. You can use filters to restrict your search to certain types of grantmakers. For a subscription fee, you can access databases with information about 80,000 grantmakers and 500,000 grants.

The Chronicle of Philanthropy has a subscription-based database that includes information about all foundation and corporate grants published in that publication since 1995. If you are a subscriber to the print version (a must read for all who need to, or want to, follow what is happening in the nonprofit sector), you can use the search engine free for searches involving the last two issues.

Government Grants

The Catalog of Federal Domestic Assistance *(http://12.46.245.173/cfda/cfda.html)* has been available free online in a searchable format since the mid-1990s. The latest version of this Web site has much more useful information for grantseekers than was available a decade ago, including a "top 10%" page that lists information about the top 10% of items in the catalog by number of "hits." Women's Business Ownership Assistance, administered by the Small Business Administration, was number one at the time we looked at this in January 2006.

Consider government grant sites

Grants.gov, launched in October 2003, takes the online search for federal government funding to a higher level. The objective of this site is to level the playing field so all eligible organizations, regardless of their size or grantsmanship sophistication, can have a fair opportunity to receive federal grants. The site directs grant seekers to funding programs offered by 26 grant-making federal agencies that aggregately award over $400 billion annually to state and local governments, academia, not-for-profits, and other organizations. It not only makes it easier for organizations to find grants of interest, but also streamlines the paperwork needed to apply for them and permits the entire process to be conducted online. All application forms, financial report data in support of agency audit and performance measurement activities, grant management procedures, and information about grant programs have been standardized across these participating agencies.

The site hosts everything an organization needs to find, apply, and manage a federal grant. Even grant notifications are made electronically. Site visitors download forms, work on them offline, and then submit completed applications electronically, saving hours of time and money. The site is divided into sections that help you engage in a six-step process, consisting of finding grant opportunities of interest, downloading the grant application package, registering with a Central Contract Registry, registering with a credentials provider, registering with grants.gov to submit grant applications, and logging on. There is even a toll-free number to use to request assistance. This site is the first place to go if you have any interest in federal grant funds.

Other places to look for information about federal government grants include—

> http://www.access.gpo.gov/
> su_docs/aces/fr-cont.html
> http://www.fundsnetservices.com/
> gov01.htm
> http://www.nonprofit.gov

> **Corporate fundraising presents many opportunities for the savvy online fundraiser, including—**
>
> - **corporate sponsorship of Web pages using banner ads and sponsor links**
> - **in-kind donation opportunities**
> - **cause marketing collaborations and partnerships**
> - **workplace giving programs**

Don't forget that many states, counties, and individual municipalities also make grants to nonprofit organizations. They often have searchable Web sites that can help in identifying funding opportunities.

Finding Corporate Support

Corporate funding sources that are not foundations do not file a 990. However, there are databases, some free and some subscription, which permit you to check them out as well. Among them are EDGAR *(http://www.sec.gov/edgar/searchedgar/webusers.htm)* and Hoover's *(http://www.hoovers.com)*. Edgar includes all filings of publicly-traded companies with the SEC since 1994. The annual filing, form 10-K, includes a lot of basic financial information, some of which may be of use to fundraisers. Hoover's includes information on both public and private companies. Some of the basic information can be viewed for free, but more detailed documents and databases require a subscription. There are other, less well known, sources for information about corporations of use to grantseekers, such as David Lamb's Prospect Research Page *(http://www.lambresearch.com/CorpsExecs.htm)*, which has plenty of links to corporate information. You can also find corporation information at Yahoo! (see *http://finance.yahoo.com).*

Of course, you will want to visit the corporation's Web site and learn more about its products and services, financial information, annual reports, newsletters that may provide details about how the organization is involved in its community, and biographies of key leadership.

Find in-kind donations

One thing that distinguishes corporate giving from its non-business counterparts is the willingness to make in-kind donations of company-produced products. Corporations give a staggering amount of products to charity. According to a survey of 150 of the largest corporations conducted by the *Chronicle of Philanthropy,* as much as 30% of total giving by these organizations consisted of in-kind gifts, more than $1 billion in 1999. The same survey conducted five years later found that two individual companies, Pfizer and Merck, have each reached or exceeded this amount in in-kind donations. Among other companies that achieved in-kind donation totals annually reaching nine figures were Johnson and Johnson, Safeway, Time-Warner, Microsoft, Bristol-Myers Squibb, and IBM.

Several intermediary Web sites have sprung up to find matches between corporations willing to provide such in-kind donations and charities that can put the products to good use. In 2004, Gifts-in-Kind *(http://www.giftsinkind.org)* alone distributed an estimated $820 million worth of goods, partnering with firms such as Office Depot, Gillette, IBM, Avon, and General Motors (each of which was honored with a "Light of Hope" Award for its efforts). According to Gifts-in-Kind, more than 200,000 charities benefited from these donations. The Web site provides an easy way for 501(c)(3) organizations to register, and there is an annual registration fee (the 2007 fee ranges from $300-$575, depending on the size of the annual budget of the organization, with a $250 fee for national charity local affiliates), as well as shipping and handling costs to receive goods.

> **A 2005 study by the Conference Board found that 189 large U.S. companies that were surveyed donated a total of $7.87 billion worldwide in 2004, more than half (56 percent) with merchandise rather than money.**

Many organizations depend on corporate support. Corporate investment in nonprofits is based on entirely different motivations from individual philanthropy.

Corporations are looking for mutual benefits. Some corporations support programs in their communities hoping that community building activity will strengthen and support their workforce. Others seek marketing benefits and value associations with organizations whose cause and good name will encourage consumers to purchase their products or services. Corporate fundraisers need to be skilled and knowledgeable in both building good relationships with corporations and helping their organizations think creatively about how they can benefit commercial enterprises.

Design your Web site to facilitate corporate support

Perhaps the Internet's primary value for corporate philanthropy is in visitor traffic. The fundraiser's Internet strategy must touch on both the organization's Web site and the corporation's. Banner ad space or recognition of corporate sponsors on an organization's Web site is important. Conversely, allowing companies to use your logo and name on their site will have a similar beneficial value, spreading the name of your organization and information about its mission to the company's stakeholders.

Some organizations develop a corporate sponsors page, typically linking logos to the corporation's Web site. These can link specifically to pages at the company's site that talk about your work, creating a "two-way street" for Web surfers. The company page might focus on the link between the particular product or service and the organization's mission. For example, a company selling baby care products might wish to be identified with an organization providing services related to infant health or child welfare.

These relationships tend to be active partnerships. Therefore, a Web strategy should be particularly dynamic—relating perhaps the regular progress toward the organization's goals with the success of the fundraising relationship.

Employee Giving Programs

Another form of corporate giving is the employee giving program. Companies with large numbers of employees may encourage them to support a particular organization with which they have a relationship. Employees may give individually or participate in fundraising events. Large nonprofits may also seek support from their own employees.

Because workplace giving operates as a special campaign, it may be worth creating a separate Web page for this, including integrating the option to give online and reporting progress to date toward a particular goal.

Resources

FirstGov.gov
http://www.firstgov.gov/Business/Business_Gateway.shtml

This site's strength lies in its convenient and user-friendly links to federal departments and agencies—executive, legislative, and judicial—and an easy-to-use guide to accessing publications of importance to nonprofits, such as the *Federal Register,* the *Catalog of Federal Domestic Assistance,* and access to the General Services Administration. It has a grid of federal agencies that permits easy access to each agency's home page, as well as a page on grants. Its search page can find information from more than a million government Web pages.

Foundation Center Online Courses Learning Lab/Virtual Courseroom
http://foundationcenter.org/getstarted/training/online/

You can take free and low-cost e-courses here to learn the basics of applying for grants, how to find funding sources, and the role of foundations in philanthropy.

Fund-Raising.com
http://www.fund-raising.com/frcboardphp/

Here you can find a message board to seek and give advice about fundraising ideas. The site's owners say that it is an information source dedicated to helping those looking for information about fundraising, and you certainly can find it there! Site sponsors are mostly for-profit companies looking for charities to purchase their products and services. For example, we found a banner ad for a company that sells custom-printed silicone rubber bracelets (similar to those distributed by the Livestrong Foundation) and another for more conventional chocolate, magazine, and cookie dough sales.

The Fundraising Bank
http://www.fundraising-ideas.com/

This site is a directory of hundreds of products that companies offer to help nonprofit organizations raise money. You can subscribe to a free monthly electronic newsletter here (click on "nonprofit resources" at the bottom of the home page). You can request information from any particular vendor by using an online product information request form at: *http://www.fundraising-ideas.com/ fundraisers/request.html*

Grants.Gov
http://www.grants.gov

The site hosts everything an organization needs to find, apply for, and manage a federal grant from a database of $400 billion worth of awards. Twenty-six federal agencies have collaborated to eliminate many of the hassles of applying for federal money.

SeaCoast WebDesign Online Grant Writing Tools
http://www.npguides.org/faqs.htm

Here you can find a free grant writing guide in .pdf format that will tell you how to put together a preliminary proposal and full proposal with a budget, with access to two sample proposals—one for foundation funding and one from government.

University of Wisconsin-Madison Grants Information Center—Databases
http://grants.library.wisc.edu/organizations/computers.html

Here you can find links to free and paid databases, both in Wisconsin and around the nation, that are useful in identifying potential sources of grants.

The MissionFish home page at: http://www.missionfish.org. Reprinted with permission. See a review of this Web site on page 99.

The Hunger Site home page at: http://www.thehungersite.com/. Reprinted with permission. See a review of this Web site on page 98.

White Hat Communications

Chapter 6

Online Fundraising Strategies

In addition to the obvious "donate here" link on your organization's Web site, there are new business models that facilitate online fundraising. Among them are creating partnerships with businesses who will provide the charity with funds in exchange for marketing opportunities, holding online charitable auctions, soliciting tribute gifts, creating online shopping malls, and engaging in search engine marketing—which involves placing advertisements on search engine Web sites that will appear on the search engine query results of those searching on a term related to the organization's mission. For each of these, there are for-profit application service providers (ASPs) to whom organizations can outsource all of the work. Many charities that engage in these strategies do this work in-house.

"Donate Here" Buttons

One obvious way charities have raised funds is by placing a "donate here" link on their Web site's pages. Clicking on the button links the donor to a secure page (i.e., where the information sent by the donor is encrypted). The page will have an online form that permits the donor to make a contribution and pay by credit card. It will typically also have information about other methods for making donations, such as a form that can be mailed or faxed to the organization, a telephone number to call during business hours to make donations, and information about planned giving. It may also have an offer for a modest "thank you" gift for donors, such as a mug with the organization's logo, a calendar, or a t-shirt.

The page should provide the donor information you need to process the donation, such as payment information, address, telephone number, and e-mail address. The page should also include information such as the organization's address and telephone number, which the donor needs to mail in a check or call in a donation. Even for those donors who do not choose to take advantage of making an online donation, it is useful to request those donors' e-mail addresses on the donation form.

Even for those organizations without merchant accounts to process credit cards or an application service provider who will (see Chapter 8 and Chapter 12), a clearly visible "donate here" button can link to a page that can be printed out and mailed with a check.

Cause-Related Marketing (CRM)

In her 1999 book, *Cause Related Marketing—Who Cares Wins*, Sue Adkins defined cause-related marketing as "commercial activity by which a business with a product, service or image to market builds a relationship with a cause or a number of causes for mutual benefit." While the term is relatively new, cause-related marketing efforts are often traced back to the 1960s, when the Insurance Company of America offered to make a donation to CARE for every insurance policy it sold. It reached prominence, however, by virtue of a well-publicized effort of American Express begun in 1983, when it pledged to donate a penny to the Statue of Liberty restoration fund for each time its card was used to make a purchase. According to press reports, this strategy was successful in increasing card use by 28% in a single year while raising substantial funds for the Statue of Liberty restoration project.

Since then, scores of mainstream charities have partnered with for-profits to exploit their brandnames and raise funds. CRM is not without controversy. A joke continues to circulate about this exploitation: Some see it as "tainted" money, while others see it as " 't ain't enough." Regardless, CRM collaborations are raising millions of dollars for charities, including the American Lung Association, the American Cancer Society, and our personal favorite—the recipients of the $.10 General Mills donates to our kids' schools when we buy their cereal with the "Box Tops for Education" coupons on the top.

Involve celebrities in cause marketing efforts

In some cases, cause-related marketing can involve three partners—the organization, the corporation, and a celebrity spokesperson. The fundraiser is looking for a good synergy that may influence everyone. A celebrity may want to help a good cause, but may also appreciate positive publicity and a boost to his or her public image. The corporation is seeking increased revenues, brand loyalty, and a positive corporate image. The charity is looking for revenues and increased awareness among the general public.

Relationships built around cause related marketing can be long-term. A good Internet strategy can help cement and maintain the relationship over time. Via e-mail, Web pages, and electronic newsletters, charities can communicate with their stakeholders about these cause-related marketing opportunities.

Online Auctions

With only a modest investment, substantial funds can be raised by offering goods and services to the public using online auction software, or using the services of a provider that administers online auctions. Charities can often obtain items, such as donated artifacts from celebrities, that are valuable to millions who may never have heard of the charity or may not specifically care about its mission. They will make a bid because of their interest in the items themselves.

Here are some online charity auction successes:

- Frederick's of Hollywood sponsored a November 2005 online auction of corsets designed and autographed by celebrities, with proceeds benefiting the Tuberous Sclerosis Alliance.

- In October 2005, the U.S. computer and video game industry raised a record $1 million to support organizations that improve the welfare of America's children from a combination of its annual black-tie dinner and an online auction.

- An X-Files online fan club raised more than $100,000 for charity. The Gillian Anderson Web Site *(http://www.gilliananderson.ws)* scheduled its eighth annual online auction in 2005, raising $23,000 (read an account of the auction at: *http://www.nfinc.org/nfinkSumFall05.pdf)*. Its previous auctions raised a total of $600,000 for Anderson's favorite charity, Neurofibromatosis, Inc.

- TV personality Ellen DeGeneres raised $25,000 for Peace Games by auctioning off a customized Vespa.

- General Motors raised over $137,000 for the SAE Foundation for Science and Technology Education by auctioning the second Chevy SSR off its production line.

- The *Today Show* raised $83,000 for Project A.L.S. by selling its *Green Room Book* on eBay.

- The National Hockey League Players' Association and National Hockey League online jersey auction raised more than $335,000 in November 2005 to support those affected by Hurricane Katrina. Among the jerseys bid on were those of Pittsburgh Penguins rookie phenom Sidney Crosby, worn in Crosby's second NHL game, which fetched almost $20,000.

You can find a listing of some current charitable online auctions at: *http://www01.charityfolks.com/charity_home.asp*

Simply searching on the term "online charity auction" using the Google search engine returns almost 100,000 hits.

Before engaging in an online auction, charities should—

- **Decide if the work will be done in-house or utilizing an application service provider**
- **Designate who will be responsible for obtaining the items, taking digital pictures of them, arranging publicity, managing order fulfillment, and managing the auction**
- **Plan how to drive traffic to their online charity auction Web pages**
- **Handling the paperwork, such as billing, receipts, thank-yous to donors and purchasers, tax collection (if required), and bookkeeping**

There are a number of advantages of having an online auction compared to conducting an auction in real time.

- You can auction off an almost infinite number of items.
- The auction can last for hours or months.
- Everyone can participate, even if they would not have found the time convenient for a conventional auction.
- People can participate from all over the world.
- The design and administration of the online auction can be performed online, providing homebound volunteers, or those busy during traditional business or meeting hours, with an opportunity to volunteer their services.
- Turnkey operations (see below) abound to assist you in startup.

Consider ASPs to manage the "backoffice"

Scores of "Dot Com" for-profit companies are competing for the right to host charitable auctions, and many provide these services free-of-charge to charities. Each for-profit host is different, and charities should be choosy and informed about the advantages and disadvantages of each. Some hosts, such as Yahoo!, provide their "backoffice" services transparently, so donors can visit the charity's Web site and access all the information they need to participate. This requires the charity to actively generate traffic to its auction site, arrange item categories, and make sure the items auctioned get to where they need to be. Other hosts can provide a soup-to-nuts menu of services, but generate Web hits for the commercial partner (and its advertisers) rather than the charity.

Consider MissionFish to set up your online charity auction

One application service provider that is gaining a reputation as the leader in online charity auctions is MissionFish *(http://www.missionfish.com)*. MissionFish, formed in 2000, is a program of the Points of Light Foundation. Charities can register and run a charity auction using the tools on this site in the same way that members of the public do.

In November 2003, MissionFish launched a program that permits the more than 135 million eBay users to donate from 10-100% of their proceeds from items sold on eBay to a favorite 501(c)(3) organization. The charity must register to be eligible to receive these donations, but registration is free. According to the Web site, more than 2,700 nonprofits have registered to benefit. As of the end of 2005, MissionFish charged a processing fee of about $3 per donation plus a 2.9% fee for credit card processing. The fee is waived up to an annual aggregate of $2 million annually for certain transactions when the seller agrees to submit at least 90% of the purchase price to a designated charity.

Participating charities have online tools to review the types of goods being auctioned off. Why is this a useful feature? As one MissionFish press release points out, a charity that is dedicated to the protection of animals wouldn't want to be the beneficiary of an auction of fur coats! Charities benefit not only from the donation, but also from the exposure of having their names listed at the auction site. There are administrative fees involved for processing, but it is possible for a charity to encourage its stakeholders to participate in this form of auction, which requires no work for the charity other than cashing the checks.

Reading some of the online testimonials *(http://www.missionfish.org/About/aboutwhatpeoplesay.jsp)* provides some ideas for charities that want to take advantage of this service. One charity executive writes that some in kind gifts were actually "unkind gifts," and MissionFish converted these unwanted goods into cash. A thrift store operator found that the revenue from the sale of one particular good online was scores of times more than what would have been received from a store sale.

Charity auction tips

What does it cost to run an online charity auction? With a bit of ingenuity, a charity auction can be administered using eBay for just a few dollars.

Here are some of our suggestions for running an online charity auction through a commercial provider.

- If you have the expertise, keep the portal for your organization's charity auction on your own Web site, creating an online community and keeping hits from potential donors on your site, not that of a commercial provider.

- Take pictures of the items you have for auction and post these online.

- Don't restrict publicity of your auction to online notices, electronic mailing lists, and e-mail. Use PSAs, newsletters, your local newspapers, snail mail postcards, and conventional publicity flyers.

- Send e-mail thank-yous to those who are the successful bidders. Mail out the items to successful bidders promptly, along with the required substantiation letter.

- If you are contracting out your charity auction to an online commercial service, review and follow our advice with respect to application service providers in Chapter 8. At the risk of being repetitive, ask lots of questions. Know exactly what your commitments and responsibilities are with respect to the agreement or contract. Direct your questions not only to the auction staff, but to other charities that have used the commercial host.

- Don't commit your organization to pay anything for participating unless you are sure that such payments are appropriate and reasonable. Many host companies do not charge anything up front to the charity, instead making their profit on a commission based on the proceeds of the auction. You will have to expend some resources to change your organization's Web site to accommodate the auction and send out promotional materials. If up front fees are charged, make sure these services are not typically provided elsewhere for free.

- Understand how and when your organization will receive its payments from successful bidders.

In summary, charity auctions are a great strategy for generating significant donations and getting people in-

---

The Internet facilitates tribute gifts by—

- **assisting in keeping track of donations**
- **communicating with donors in a sensitive way**
- **providing low-cost, attractive recognition to donors and those they honor**

volved in a charity and educated about its mission and focus. But it takes some work and creativity.

Tribute Gifts

Tributes are memorial gifts given in the name of a loved one, usually shortly after they die. Tribute gifts encourage family and friends to join together, and sometimes hundreds participate. Most fundraising offices do not have staff dedicated solely to tributes. Instead, they are folded into the work of other fundraisers, either in major gifts, direct marketing, special events, or other specialist or generalist fundraisers.

We mention tributes here because they often provide a particular challenge. Managing tribute gifts can be highly labor intensive. Often, the size of the tribute is not proportional to the amount of work it requires. Gifts need to be meticulously tracked and recorded. Communications need to be sent to the donors and to the family, keeping them apprised of each contributor and the total.

Soliciting tribute gifts requires sensitivity

While tributes are always highly valued and appreciated, fundraisers can see them as difficult to manage and distracting to the more proactive fundraising they are charged with doing. Smoothly managing tribute funds often goes unpraised, while the slightest error draws unwelcome attention and consequences. What manager wants to hear a complaint from a family at this deeply emotional time of their lives?

Furthermore, fundraisers have long sensed the potential to increase fundraising around tributes, but struggle with how to sensitively make an approach. Many of the largest gifts honor a lost loved one, but tribute gifts happen when a family isn't focused on philanthropy. The timing for discussing what the family could do is the worst possible, usually taking place around the funeral of a loved one. And often the connection, if there was any, was with the deceased, making it hard to re-engage with family members after enough time has passed. So, too often, the family and the organization part ways after a tribute fund is established, despite the possibility of greater support.

One new approach by Our Lasting Tribute *(http://ourlastingtribute.com)* seems interesting to us and may represent a creative way to use the Internet to increase giving through a culture shift in traditional philanthropy. Although this company utilizes written materials in its approach, as well as the Internet, we will focus on the role of the Internet here.

Imagine that a family wishing to establish a tribute did so through the creation of a mini-campaign online. Automated technology can allow a donor to set up a Web page connected to your organization's. At this Web site, the family can put pictures and details about their loved one and why they have designated your organization as their charity of choice. Others visiting could add their own thoughts, poems, prayers, and memories, and at the same time pledge their support to the fund.

Set up an online tribute page

An online tribute page can alleviate many of the managerial headaches of tribute funds while maximizing their potential and respecting the needs of the family at a difficult time. Visitors automatically know the exact fundraising total. Family members can be informed of gifts through e-mail, and while some paper acknowledgment and receipt is still needed, e-mail versions can help cut down significantly on problems, perceived or real, and in doing so, reduce the number of complaints. Because this Internet approach encourages families to come back to the question of philanthropy later, after the most difficult and immediate emotionally absorbing event, it can help resolve some of the timing and appropriateness issues associated with fundraising for tributes.

In short, the Internet may hold a key to helping to unlock the untapped potential in tribute funds. It can help to empower families to do more and to take greater satisfaction in the impact they are having in the name of a loved one. This may in turn lead to more substantial relationships with such families, and in some cases may even transform them into lifelong supporters or major donors.

Personal Fundraising Pages

Donors, be they casual or wealthy philanthropists, are more likely to give when asked by someone they know, or to whom they have some connection. Colleges and universities ask current students to volunteer to solicit alumni. Charities provide their supporters with donor materials, and ask that they mail solicitations to their neighbors with a personalized appeal. Organizations hold galas and other special events and encourage the well-heeled to invite their friends to attend, or to make a contribution if they cannot be there in person.

The technology revolution has added new wrinkles to many existing fundraising techniques, eliminating some labor-intensive aspects, and streamlining invitations, donor processing, acknowledgment and substantiation, and collections. Technology has also spurred the development of new, creative fundraising models. Among them are charity malls, online auctions, "click-to-give," and electronic tribute gifts. Some of these models take advantage of using "personal" appeals of individuals to their friends, neighbors, and relatives, despite the fact that these appeals are highly automated and involve minimal labor on the part of either the charity or the solicitor.

One such model, the individual fundraising page, is rapidly catching on as an effective fundraising technique for charities on the cutting edge. It was successful recently in generating a donation from one of us, Gary Grobman, to a charity that he had not previously supported, the Leukemia and Lymphoma Society. Here's how it occurred.

ASPs can manage personal fundraising pages

In January 2005, Gary Grobman received an e-mail from a casual friend and neighbor, Shalom Staub of Harrisburg, PA. The message, not particularly long or detailed, said Shalom was participating in a 100-mile bike ride around Lake Tahoe in June to raise millions of dollars for this particular charity, and he was committed to raising $3,800 himself. He asked for Gary's participation by clicking on a link embedded in his e-mail. The link was to Shalom's personal fundraising page on Active.com. Gary complied, making a small donation online. Within minutes, he received two e-mails, one from the local chapter of the charity thanking him for his gift, and a receipt from the application service provider, Active.com. Apparently, scores of others responded to the appeal. In July, Gary received another "custom" e-mail from his biker friend saying that over 1,900 bike riders raised $7 million, and that he more than met his fundraising goal. Attached to the e-mail were pictures of the event.

Active.com is a site managed by Active Giving Solutions, one of many application service providers who have developed software applications for personal fundraising pages. "We chose Active Giving Solutions for its customized technology and ability to integrate with our internal systems," said Richard J. Geswell, executive vice president, marketing and revenue generation for the Leukemia & Lymphoma Society, in a June 2005 press release. "We needed an easy tool to encourage and expand online fundraising by our participants. With Active's history of managing online transactions for participatory sports and its ties to the active lifestyle community, we're also looking forward to the additional exposure we gain through the partnership."

Perhaps the leader in the personal fundraising page model is Justgiving.com, with more than a million online donations received for its 1,200 nonprofit organization clients in the United States and Great Britain in its first five years of operations. A March 2005 survey of more than 1,000 Justgiving users validated the company's claim that making donations via this method is convenient, secure, and provides many other advantages over conventional methods of solicitation. One satisfied customer, Nathaniel Tilton, was diagnosed with Multiple Sclerosis in 2002. Rather than being impeded by his debilitating disease, he set a goal of running the Boston Marathon. Setting up his personal fundraising page on Justgiving.com, he raised more than $10,000 for his charity and finished the race in a respectable 4:43 on a hot day and challenging course (and likely passed Gary Grobman somewhere after Heartbreak Hill).

To Shalom Staub, this automated service relieved much of the anxiety and time involved in fundraising.

"Some people who were distant to me, or who only knew of me through a friend or family member, donated quite generously," he told Gary in an e-mail. "Others who are closer friends of mine, failed to, which was frustrating. The point is, you just never know who might feel a personal connection to your cause and who might be willing to make a contribution—so don't be afraid to ask!"

The technology made his plea for support painless at every step. The cost to charities is reasonable, with typical transaction fees being 5% or less of donations made through the Justgiving platform. From the home page *(http:// www.justgiving.com),* you can find the personal fundraising pages of some of the top fundraisers who use the service, and the names and comments of their donors.

Also started in 1999, CharityFocus *(http://www.charityfocus.org)* is a California-based 501(c)(3) that is run completely by volunteers. Its basic services, including setting up personal fundraising pages (see: *http://www.pledgepage.org),* are free, although there may be charges for any third-party costs the organization incurs on your behalf.

Third party application service providers are becoming more sophisticated in meeting the customized needs of charities that want to encourage their donors to set up personal fundraising pages. Typically, these pages permit the participant to upload pictures, provide progress reports on the amount of donations received, and have colorful graphics that illustrate how close the participant is to meeting his or her fundraising goal. Anecdotal evidence is strong that charities, participants, and donors alike appreciate the convenience of this online giving option. And it is another effective strategy charities can use to add to their donor lists and publicize the important mission they have, even among those who may not be interested in making a donation.

Online Shopping Malls

Just imagine. Instead of going to their favorite mall to purchase a national brand product, your charity's friends and supporters go online and visit a Web site that charges them the customary (and often discounted) price, and funnels a percentage of the purchase price directly to your charity. Their purchases from retailers and discounters such as Toys R Us, Amazon.com, and Sharper Image are delivered on their doorstep within a day or two, and your charity receives a check aggregating all of these donations, no strings attached.

This is not the future.

This scenario is occurring thousands of times each day on scores of Web sites, and the number of such transactions is expanding exponentially. Online retailing accounted for just .5% of purchases made in 1998, but climbed to 1.2% in one year. David Schatsky, senior vice president of research at JupiterResearch, reported that for 2005, U.S. online retail sales would reach $79 billion, versus $66 billion in 2004.

> *Fundraising tip:* **Organizations that are most successful in attracting donors to their Web sites purchase appropriate keywords from major search engines to ensure that they appear when potential donors try to find them. They also track the responses to the key words they purchase, in order to understand how often each is used. Each keyword purchased can also be directed to a particular place within the organization's Web site. Some organizations even purchase common misspellings of keywords!**

Online shopping malls compete

Intense competition is just beginning among for-profit entrepreneurs who seek to obtain the cooperation of charities in directing traffic to their sites. We think that this development is very positive for both charities and consumers, although both need to be aware of limitations and potential problems associated with this trend.

Many in the charitable community have had a love-hate relationship with the private sector. We benefit from the generosity of grants and donations from capitalist enterprises, while at the same time we denigrate the exploitation and lack of altruism inherent in rampant commercialism and consumerism. After all, many charities (and government programs, as well) were initiated because of the failure of the market to address many human needs.

Some of the entrepreneurs who have initiated these collaborative programs with charities have a genuine desire to parlay their commercial success into socially responsible activities that benefit society. And others, no doubt, cynically recognize that they can generate revenue by serving as middlemen and reaching a new market of consumers attracted by the incentive of helping their favorite charity. Regardless of the reasons motivating these "dot-com" companies, the advent of e-commerce has seen a proliferation of for-profit Web sites geared toward combining the joys of shopping with the imperative of helping the less fortunate. They are probably here to stay.

Among the prominent charity-shopper sites are (in alphabetical order):

Benevolink *(http://www.benevolink.com/)*
Charitymall.com *(http://www.charitymall.com)*
GreaterGood.com *(http://www.greatergood.com)*
iGive.com *(http://www.igive.com)*
Mycause.com *(http://www.mycause.com)*
Working Assets *(http://www.workingassets.com/shop/)*

Search Engine Marketing (SEM)

Studies show that 80-85% of initial visits to a Web site begin with a query to a search engine. This astounding statistic illustrates how important it is for charities to build and develop a successful search engine marketing and optimization campaign, which includes placing metatags in HTML to enhance search engine results placement, purchasing paid ads from search engines based on keywords you select, having lots of links to your site (which can affect search engine ranking), and adding new content to increase traffic to your site as much as possible.

In March 2003, there was an interesting article in the *Chronicle of Philanthropy* about a partnership between the international aid organization, Childreach, and the producer of the movie *About Schmidt*. The movie was about a retired insurance executive who "sponsored" a seven-year-old child from Tanzania with his donations to Childreach. The article documented some of the steps taken by the charity to exploit the publicity generated by the movie to increase its fundraising—including signing a contract with the producers that provided benefits to both parties.

Buried deep in the article is a lesson that every charity should consider when developing its Internet marketing plan. While Childreach engaged in substantial direct mail and telephone soliciting coordinated with the message in this Oscar-winning movie, a competing charity found a way to reach potential donors who had an interest in the movie. Children International purchased Google AdWords on the popular search engine. When people searched on the term "About Schmidt," the search engine provided a link to Children International, urging them to "make a difference" by sponsoring a child.

For-profit businesses have been engaging in search engine marketing (SEM) strategies routinely for several years. But it has been only recently that charities have recognized the return on their investment provided by establishing partnerships with companies such as Google *(http://www.google.com),* Yahoo! Search Marketing *(http://searchmarketing.yahoo.com/index.php)* and Enhance *(http://www.enhance.com).*

Even common misspellings pay dividends

The December 26, 2004 tsunami disaster mobilized scores of international relief organizations to implement strategies to take advantage of the outpouring of donors and potential donors to do something fast to help. Within hours of the disaster, using Google to search on the term "Tsunami" resulted in user screens showing paid links to organizations such as World Vision, UNICEF-USA, Save the Children, and the American Red Cross. We even found paid advertisements for Direct Relief and MercyCorps when we intentionally put the misspelled word "sunami" into the search engine form.

What are the results? Rick Christ of NPAdvisors.com, an online fundraising consulting group, reports that—

"One of our clients got to work with us Sunday, Dec. 26 (2004), even though they were also being hit with a one-foot snowstorm near them. They authorized a keyword buy and began working on an e-mail to sponsors. The keywords produced over 34,000 visits to their tsunami relief page between December 27 and January 18 and together with the e-mail they have raised about ten times their normal December amount online, mostly in the last few days of the month. The keywords have helped generate over 600 new online donors to their cause."

How do you start an SEM campaign? Here are three basic steps.

Step 1: Research the sites that offer this service. While Google and YAHOO! Search Marketing dominate this industry, competing programs are offered by Enhance *(http://www.enhance.com/)*, Kanoodle *(http://www.kanoodle.com)*, and MIVA *(http://www.miva.com.us)*. There is minimal standardization on how these programs work. Google, for example, lets you set what you are willing to pay based on a daily budget and a maximum cost per click (CPC)—the cost the advertiser pays to the site publisher each time a visitor clicks on the advertiser's ad—and partners with AOL, CompuServe, and other high-traffic search engines.

Yahoo! Search Marketing requires a monthly budget (although you can set up an account for as little as $5) and allows you to place a bid on any keyword, but sets a minimum price of ten cents/click-through—defined as when a Web page visitor clicks on an ad and that visitor's browser exits the page on which the ad appeared and enters the Web site linked to in the ad—and also sets a maximum bid price. You can use a tool on the site to search on a prospective keyword and see what the current bid is. Its main search engine clients are its parent company, YAHOO!, Lycos, and Alta Vista.

Step 2: *Identify the keywords that are the most likely to help search engines find you (such as for use in metatags—which are hidden HTML tags containing the page's title, description, and keywords that are used by search engines to index pages but don't appear on the Web page—and the keywords that will help those who use search engines find your site.* Your brainstorming needs to focus on the most likely words people will use in their search engine submission, considering that they may not have heard of your organization, and their initial search may not be particularly targeted to finding you, but rather some general information about something directly or indirectly related to your organization's mission. One useful site that will help you is Wordtracker *(http://www.wordtracker.com)*. This London-based site will give you statistics on how often people who use search engines search on particular terms. This is a fee-based subscription service, but you can subscribe for as little as one day for less than $10, and the company offers a full money-back guarantee any time within the first 30 days if you subscribe.

Step 3. *Do the preliminary work required before making the purchase.* This includes preparing a budget, identifying the keywords to purchase, redesigning your site, if necessary, and making sure the pages linked to by the ad are consistent with the advertising copy in the ads.

Step 4: *Make the purchase.* Major SEM sites provide clear instructions, making it easy to begin your marketing effort virtually instantaneously, provided you have a major credit card.

Can't afford to buy an ad? Google has established a program called "Google Grants" to provide free AdWords to 501(c)(3) tax-exempt organizations that share Google's values, particularly those with missions in the areas of science and technology, education, global public health, environment, youth advocacy, and the arts. Google Grants makes its awards to about 300 organizations each quarter, and each receives at least three months of this in-kind donation. To apply, you can fill out an online form available at: *http://www.google.com/grants.* Organizations will need to provide sample keywords, ad copy, and a statement of how they will benefit from their participation. Organizations already participating in the Google AdSense program are ineligible.

Search engine marketing is only one of many emerging, innovative strategies to increase your organization's reach to potential donors. While it does, in most cases, require some up front investment, the ROI is among the best of any that can be found in the toolbox of the online fundraiser.

Resources

Active.com
http://www.active.com

Active.com is a site managed by Active Giving Solutions, one of many application service providers with software applications for personal fundraising pages.

Auction Anything
http://www.auctionanything.com/

AuctionAnything is a for-profit application service provider that offers more types of auction services than MissionFish. The company charges a one-time setup fee in addition to hosting and maintenance fees, but does not charge commissions on sales.

Bpath
http://www.bpath.com

You can download free tools to upgrade your Web site in order to increase traffic, such as site visit counters, tell-a-friend buttons, banners, e-mail forms, and message boards.

CharityFocus
http://www.charityfocus.org

This is a California-based 501(c)(3), developed in 1999, that is run completely by volunteers. If your organization doesn't currently have a Web presence, but wants to develop an online fundraising program, this is the first site you should visit. Read the FAQ at: *http://www.cfsites.org/index.php?pg=faq*

Charitygift
http://www.kintera.org/site/c.hjITI3PHKoG/b.569023/k.CB6A/Home.htm

This innovative business model to encourage charitable donations is a for-profit venture that permits the public to custom-design birthday, wedding, sympathy, Bar Mitzvah, and other types of cards online using templates. The purchaser includes a charitable donation in honor of the recipient, choosing any one of 680,000 charities. The vendor sends the card by snail mail or e-mail, and funnels 100% of the donation to the charity. The fee to the donor for the service starts from $3.95 per card, depending on quantity, plus a 5% credit card transaction fee. An acknowledgment is sent to the donor by e-mail immediately.

Charitymall.com
http://www.charitymall.com

This is one of the few sites that pledge to pass along 100% of the rebates to the designated charity, the Cancer Research Foundation. Commissions provided by the more than 100 merchants range from 1-50% and are posted on the site. The home page describes the "typical" rebate as "3-30%." Purchasers must set up a separate e-mail account for transactions with merchants in order for donations to be credited to charities, and the purchasers must have a separate account for each charity they designate for the rebate. Charities can download promotional materials from the site's sponsor.

Free Online Surveys
http://www.freeonlinesurveys.com

According to the site, the free account allows you to create a questionnaire of up to 20 questions and receive up to 50 responses over a 10-day period, with standard accounts costing $19.95/month with discounts for students and teachers.

The Hunger Site
http://www.thehungersite.com

Visit this example of a vibrant "click-to-give" site and click on the "Donate Free Food" icon that results in the site sponsors making a donation to a food bank, joining almost a quarter-of-a-million others daily. Each sponsor pays one half cent per donation, which buys a quarter cup of food. When we clicked last, there were ten sponsors, whose banner ads appear after the click. According to information on the site, more than 14,000 metric tons of food have been donated as the result of the clicks of 150 million visitors. Click on the "shopping" icon and you are transported to an online shopping mall where up to 15% of the purchase price is donated to the UN food program.

iGive.com
http://www.igive.com

iGive.com is the venerable granddaddy of online philanthropic/shopping services, at the ripe old age of seven (as of 2006). As we write this, the service has more than 100,000 members. More than 30,000 causes have qualified for payments from iGive.com, amounting to about two million dollars (you can view recent payments on the Web site) that range from a penny to several hundred dollars. Each of the more than 600 merchants who participate negotiates an amount rebated to the charity of between .4% and 26%. All of the rebate is sent to the charity, usually within 60-90 days after the purchase is made. iGive.com receives its own commission from the merchants that is equal to or less than the amount received by the charity. The sponsors will make a $5 donation to your designated charity when you make your first purchase.

MissionFish
http://www.missionfish.org/

As of January 2006, more than 7,500 charities have registered with MissionFish, an eBay partner and part of the Points of Light Foundation. MissionFish has raised more than $20 million for participating charities through online auctions. Registered eBay users (and there are more than 135 million of them) can use MissionFish tools to donate from 10-100% of the proceeds of their auction sales to charities. The site has resources to get you started, and includes information about conference call training sessions held every other week. Accounts are free for participating nonprofits.

WebSurveyor
http://www.websurveyor.com

Here you can download free online tools to create a quick survey on your Web site or by using e-mail.

Zoomerang
http://www.zoomerang.com/web/signup/Basic.aspx

You can sign up at this URL for a free account, offering limited survey capability for free. The company offers more sophisticated software for a fee.

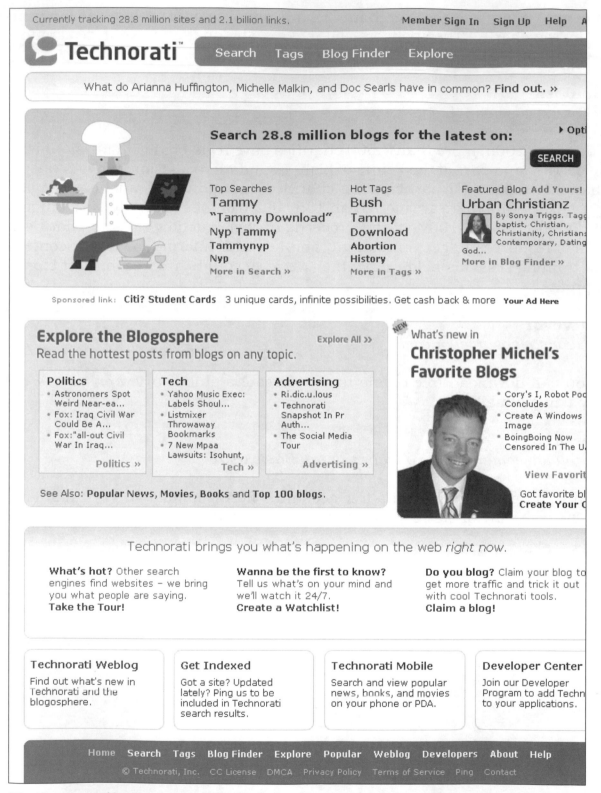

The Technorati home page at: http://www.technorati.com. Reprinted with permission. See a review of this Web site on page 109.

Chapter 7

Internet Strategies That Encourage Fundraising

Earlier in this book, we reported on success stories of charities that are raising millions of dollars online. There are many ways to make the "ask," but few require less expense than having a Web site that makes it easy to donate.

Simply having a Web site is clearly not enough to bring your organization fame, friends, and fortune. The "build it and they will come" philosophy may work well for Hollywood baseball movies, but you need to take proactive steps to build a base of loyal visitors and keep them returning.

Encouraging First-Time Visitors

Building a Web site that encourages first-time visitors has become an art form. Page design, load time, color schemes, pictures, animations, graphics, and how content is linked from one page to another based on your visitors' needs have become important issues for Web page designers.

Unique content is the key

Of primary importance to nonprofit organization Web sites, of course, is the content itself. You can safely assume that a visitor is not likely to be visiting your site to be entertained, as there are thousands of commercial sites that do that quite well. In most cases, visitors will be pointing their browsers to your organization's site because they have an interest in the organization's cause and the information is not available anywhere else, or because they were directed there by some other source.

Take advantage of that knowledge, and put content on your site that will meet the specific information needs of your visitors. If you can do this in a pleasing format, fine, but don't sacrifice the unique content only you can provide—backed by the credibility of your organization's reputation—in exchange for "bells and whistles." A simply designed site with good content can be quite effective.

We can offer additional advice for driving new traffic to your site:

Put a "Refer to a Friend" button on your home page. Part of what has become known as a "viral marketing" strategy, this allows visitors to send an e-mail to someone he or she knows. The automated format of this e-mail includes information about your site, including a link to it. Because the receiver of this message gets it from a friend and is likely to be interested in your site, that person is likely to visit it, and, perhaps, tell more friends. It is an electronic way to tell about your site using "word of mouth," or "word of mouse." You can find the code to incorporate this feature on your site at, among other places, http://send-a-link.com.

> Charities can take advantage of the interactive nature of the Web when raising funds. Charity Web sites that encourage fundraising are those that make content their first priority. These sites need to make an effort to attract first-time visitors and have features that encourage return visits.

Use metatags in your Web pages. Registering with search engines and directories doesn't guarantee that the person looking for information will find your organization in the search results instead of hundreds of others with similar information. Type the words "animal shelter" in the Google search engine and it responds with two million "hits." Viewers are not likely to browse through more than a few of these pages. You want to take steps to help the search engine give you high placement compared to competing Web pages. One way to do this is using metatags—key words and descriptions that appear in your Web page source code and are used by search engines to rank the likelihood that your particular page will be useful to the searcher. Each search engine uses a different process to calculate the placement of search results. There are sites that are helpful in explaining all of the technical details about submitting to search engines and directories, and inserting the right metatags. Among the most popular free ones are Search-Engine-Secrets.net *(http://search-engine-secrets.net/),* Stepforth *(http://news.stepforth.com/2003-news/ten-minute-optimization.shtml),* and Digital Web Magazine *(http://www.digital-web.com/articles/designing_for_search_engines_and_stars/).*

Maximize links to your Web site from other organizations. Develop a link strategy to get the message out about your site. One popular strategy is to identify Web sites that appeal to the same audiences as yours. You can do this by using search engines to search key words. Then e-mail the Webmaster for these organizations and offer to exchange links. You can have a separate "links" page on your site, with one-sentence descriptions. In this way, visitors to those sites who may not know about yours have the opportunity to visit with a simple click of the mouse.

Another form of exchanging links is participating in a Web ring. These are cooperative linkages of Web sites that have a common theme or topic. Each ring is administered by an individual Web site owner who screens requests to join the ring. For example, there are at least 23 Web rings on the topic of breast cancer. If your organization has a mission related to this topic and receives permission to join one of these rings, you will receive the appropriate code to place on your Web site. A visitor to your site and others that are members of the ring sees graphics and buttons that permit him or her to visit each site that is a member of the ring by clicking on them. This drives targeted traffic to your site from those who are visiting the sites of other members of the ring. For more information, check out *http://dir.webring.com/rw* and *http://www.ringsurf.com.*

> **To encourage first-time visitors—**
>
> - **Make your site the one place to go for unique content related to your organization's mission**
> - **Publicize the site's Internet address on all organization communications**
> - **Insert a "refer a friend" script on the home page**
> - **Register with search engines**
> - **Use metatags in your HTML coding**
> - **Encourage link exchanges**
> - **Engage in search engine marketing (SEM)**

Promote your Web site address on all organization materials. A final suggestion is to add your organization's Web site address to all of your organization's promotional items, brochures, newsletters, and conference/workshop materials. Put your site's address on your e-mail signature, your business cards, letterhead, and all of your advertisements—both print and online. It doesn't cost any more to do so, and this free advertising gets the word out.

Encouraging Repeat Web Site Visits

Changing the content often is the most important step toward keeping loyal visitors returning. This requires a commitment that consists of two parts. First, content relating to your organization's activities, upcoming events, public policy and advocacy briefings, staff responsibilities, newsletter postings, and other information should be updated at least every week—more frequently if you are able to do this. Second, you need a strategy to let everyone know when there is updated information on your site.

Many Web-savvy organizations routinely keep focused on what needs to be updated on their sites by publishing weekly newsletters that are distributed by e-mail to stakeholders who request them (see Chapter 4). You can archive back issues on your site and use the content of each newsletter as your reminder to systematically keep your conventional Web site content current.

To encourage return visitors—

- **update your content periodically**
- **offer contests, prizes, surveys, and polls on your site**
- **add features that encourage return visits, such as message boards, blogs, online auctions, chat rooms, and scrolling news about the organization and its mission**
- **add a script that allows visitors to bookmark the site**

Let visitors know about your site

Now that you've updated your site, you need to let visitors know about it. Your electronic newsletter can be the vehicle for informing your stakeholders and other site visitors of updates and new material added to your site. You can design your site with a "What's New" link that will make it easy for visitors to see what has been added recently. This can also be accomplished by putting a "NEW!" or "UPDATED!" icon beside a link to a page that was recently added or updated. It is also useful to add a line at the bottom of your home page divulging the date when the page was last updated. Doing this may even provide an incentive for you to update your page more often, so as to avoid the embarrassment of having too many days pass before any material was changed on your site. You can send an e-mail or press release to the publishers of electronic and print newsletters and electronic mailing lists informing them about the availability of new files and features on your Web site. Take advantage of all of the free promotional resources you can!

Add features to attract visitors

Experienced Webmasters know that simply adding new content and telling people about it is not always enough to encourage repeat visitors. They use a variety of techniques. For example, offer something free, such as an electronic newsletter, contests (with prizes), surveys, or a downloadable screensaver with your organization's logo and URL. If your organization sells goods and services or charges for events (see Gary Grobman's book, *The Nonprofit Organization's Guide to E-Commerce* for ideas), provide a printable coupon on your site that will give visitors a discount.

Add useful services such as a job bank, blogs, chat room, message board, or a library of informative issue papers that will encourage visitors to return again and again. Chat rooms and message boards are among the best techniques for building an online community—the ultimate goal you should have for promoting repeat visits. It is from building such an online community that an organization can substantially increase its pool of volunteers (virtual and otherwise), donors, advocates, and loyal supporters.

Use your Web site to conduct an auction of donated goods and services (see Chapter 6). This not only increases Web site traffic, but can generate supplemental revenue as well.

Ask visitors to bookmark the site, using a custom-designed bookmark icon. Bookmarking provides a convenient way for a Web browser to "remember" your site's Web address. It may not be obvious, but having your Web site in a person's "favorites list" is one of the best strategies to generate repeat visits.

PayPal Simplifies Web Payment Processing

In June 2005, PayPal, the leading online payments processor, announced a new service called "PayPal Website Payments Pro." Subscribers to this service can accept online credit card payments via their Web sites without having their own merchant accounts. PayPal provides instructions on integrating this service with the shopping cart software used by your online store. Another feature of the service allows you to take credit card information by mail, telephone, fax, or in person and process the payment through PayPal's Web site. The customer sees your organization's name on his or her credit card bill just as if you had your own merchant account. The initial fees for this service are quite reasonable, starting at $20/month, 30 cents per transaction, and a fee of from 2.2-2.9% of the transaction, depending on volume. Unlike most merchant accounts offered by financial institutions, there is no startup fee. Other high profile third-party application service providers are expected to compete for this lucrative market, which may drive fees down in the future.

How do you add these tools to your site without busting your budget? See an online article on bookmarks by Dr. Ralph Wilson, which can be found at: *http://wilsonweb.com/wmta/bookmark.htm.* Visit sites such as BraveNet *(http://www.bravenet.com/)*, Home Page Tools *(http://www.homepagetools.com/)*, Media Builder *(http://www.mediabuilder.com)*, and Mega Web Tools *(http://www.megawebtools.com)*. Keep in mind that some free services may require advertising messages from the sponsor, and you may not wish to have these appear on your site. Some may offer these services/tools without advertising, for a fee.

Your Web site should not be a stagnant pond. Rather, it needs to be a vibrant river—flourishing, animated, dynamic, and zippy—making a measurable, positive contribution to your organization's communications and public relations efforts. An investment in some time and effort in building traffic to your Web site will help you in reaching your organization's goals.

Blogs

Blogging is sweeping the online communications world. Short for "Web Log," the blog is changing the way individuals and organizations communicate to a degree rivaling the impact of Web sites. According to Lee Rainie, director of the Pew Internet & American Life Project, there are at least ten million of them, with a total readership of more than 35 million Americans. More than a hundred thousand new blogs are added each week. Technorati *(http://www.technorati.com)* now boasts that its blog search engine can find 17.5 million blogs. To compete, Google launched a new search engine in September 2005 specifically tailored to this emerging medium *(http://blogsearch.google.com)*.

The nonprofit sector, with limited exceptions, appears to be on the sidelines, missing an opportunity to take advantage of what blogging has to offer. For fundraisers, the blog offers an opportunity to share with donors and potential donors information with a "human touch" that they would not likely get from any other source, even from the traditional Web pages of the organization, with an opportunity to provide feedback in the form of comments, criticisms, suggestions, and other interaction. Nonprofit blogs are not just informative; they are entertaining to those who are interested in what staff are thinking.

What blogs are

A blog is a Web page that consists of a frequently updated journal or diary by an individual. The style of commentary is typically informal and personal, usually including links to additional online resources embedded within the content. Each entry is in reverse chronological order—the latest entry is placed on top. Each dated entry has its own Web address (called a "permalink"), making it easy for other blogs and search engines to link to any particular entry (rather than to the entire blog). Previous entries are archived on the blogger's site. There is a process that permits viewers to add their comments to each entry, which can be seen by all viewers. Many blogs have an RSS (for *Really Simple Syndication*) feed, a software application that lets viewers subscribe to blog updates by using an RSS reader, thus eliminating the requirement to visit each blog site individually to obtain access to updates of their favorites.

Blog content can be personal

In the nonprofit context, a blog might include the daily musings of an executive director of an advocacy agency, sharing her thoughts on a news development of the day, adding links to online articles that have come across her computer screen about that news, commenting on how her organization's stakeholders will be affected, providing some insight into some of the internal debate within her agency about how to deal with it, and perhaps observing how thrilled she is that her two-year-old has finally been potty-trained. Included might be vacation pictures and links to the blogs of her friends and colleagues. It is this glimpse into the staff member's personal life that gives the organizational blog its special charm, although divulging such personal information is certainly not a requirement and in some cases may be inappropriate.

Blogs are perhaps a reflection of a change in popular online culture as much as an advance in online technology. In one form or another, blogs have been around since Web sites began. What is different is the informality of posts, and the willingness of individuals to "let their hair down" and show their vulnerability.

For the nonprofit community, blogs provide another mechanism to improve interaction with an organization's stakeholders, enhance the bond with donors, and create a dialogue with outsiders while giving them an inside look at what the organization is trying to accomplish. The technical tools are easily accessible, and we encourage you to at least take a blog for a test drive and verify that the benefits to you and your organization are substantial.

Nonprofits should consider blogging

Blogs serve many purposes for a nonprofit organization. If they are interesting or provocative, they draw readership—not only from the general public, but from the media and political leadership, as well. And these site visits often translate to new and more productive current donors, volunteers, advocates, and friends. They often give more of a sense of a vibrant, active, dynamic, and HUMAN organizational life than a print newsletter/annual report or a Web page that is more like a sterile brochure than an organic, flourishing online community. Because of the ability for viewers to comment, the feedback is often invaluable to bloggers. And, according to a September 2005 study sponsored by America Online (AOL), nearly half of bloggers do so because they find it to be "therapeutic"!

Cautions about blogging

Of course, there are some disadvantages. The advice we always give to "never put anything in an e-mail that would make you uncomfortable seeing on the front page of the *New York Times*" applies to blogs, as well. To date, hundreds of employees have been fired for what they have written in blogs, for anything from bad-mouthing their organizations to disclosing confidential or proprietary information, or to writing denigrating comments about coworkers. One instructor at Boston University was canned for blogging about a "distractingly attractive student," according to one press report. Many organizations have formal, written blogging policies, spelling out what types of posts are inappropriate. Many other organizations have simply banned them.

Bloggers need to vigilantly monitor all comments, routinely deleting "comment spam" and inappropriate comments.

Examples of nonprofit organization blogs

Point your browser to: *http://www.omidyar.net/group/compumentor/ws/nonprofit_blogs/* for a directory of some nonprofit organization blogs, organized by mission category. Among those to check out for ideas on how the blog concept works and might add value to your own organization's Web site are—

Democracy in Action: *http://blog.democracyinaction.org/*
Vermont Nonprofit CommunIT: *http://cvnp.typepad.com/blog/*
Michael Gilbert's Nonprofit Online News: *http://news.gilbert.org/*

Tools for blogging

Setting up a blog is remarkably simple and inexpensive. The method that requires the least technical proficiency is using an application service provider such as Blogger *(http://new.blogger.com)* or Typepad *(http://www.typepad.com)*. Blogger is free. As of January 2006, Typepad, one of the most popular services, offers a 30-day free trial with a fee starting at less than $50/year. Each service has its advantages and disadvantages.

You can install blogging software (e.g., using WordPress, *http://www.wordpress.org* or Radio UserLand, *http://radio.userland.com),* and there are distinct advantages and disadvantages to each of these. WordPress is open source software, which means it is free and can be customized by your organization. Radio Userland can be licensed for under $40/year and offers a free trial.

For a discussion of server-installed choices, visit Blog Software Breakdown at: *http://www.asymptomatic.net/blogbreakdown.htm*

Resources

BraveNet
http://www.bravenet.com/

This is one of the best Web sites on the Net for free Web hosting services and Webbuilder tools. Here you can download free guestbooks, hit counters, chatrooms, clipart, audioclips, message boards, and all of the Web templates you need to build a smart, functioning Web site.

Google Blog Search
http://blogsearch.google.com

This site returned more than 200 hits on our March 2006 search on the term "Fundraising Online," with a lot less distracting advertising than Technorati. As this was still a Beta version, we expect this search engine will only improve and eat up all of its competition.

Home Page Tools
http://www.homepagetools.com/

Since 1998, this site has offered free, customizable Web tools, including message boards, counters, guest books, an events manager, and clip art. It claims to have more than 600,000 unique users of its services.

Media Builder
http://www.mediabuilder.com/

This commercial site offers a generous supply of free samples of clip art, photos, and animations you can use on your Web pages. A one-year membership runs $99.95 and provides access to hundreds of thousands of animations, clipart, templates, and videoclips.

Mega Web Tools
http://www.megawebtools.com/

This commercial site offers free Web building tools, including counters and stat programs, guestbooks, chatrooms, and information about free scrolling tickers that provide current news, weather, and sports.

Technorati
http://www.technorati.com

This site is the authority on Weblogs, and includes a search engine with access to more than 30 million sites with over two billion links. Our search in March 2006 on the keywords "Fundraising Online" returned 113 unique hits of blog posts.

Web Content Accessibility Guidelines Working Group
http://www.w3.org/WAI/GL/

This page links to documents describing efforts to set standards to make Web pages accessible to people with disabilities.

Web Page Backward Compatibility Viewer
http://www.delorie.com/web/wpbcv.html

This site allows you to test how various components of your Web page would look using different Web browsers.

Web Ring, Inc.
http://dir.webring.com/rw

This is a searchable site that has both a directory and search engine to help you find existing Web rings. Searching on the term "arts" turned up 25 rings.

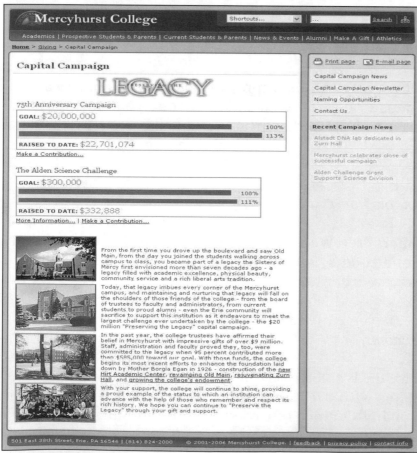

The Mercyhurst College capital gifts page at: http://www.mercyhurst.edu/giving/capital-campaign.php. Reprinted with permission.

Working With Application Service Providers

Many charities are partnering with for-profit providers that engage in creative business models designed to generate and process charitable donations. For example, "click to give" sites reward visitors who click on a link to a sponsoring business by making a modest donation to a designated charity. On other sites, individuals who agree to install special software on their computer to keep track of online retail purchases can designate a portion of the sale price to a participating charity. Another model allows online supermarket coupon bar codes that let shoppers make a donation in the amount of the coupon to be printed out, with the donation charged at the checkout line, aggregated, and sent to the charity.

There are full-service e-philanthropy companies such as Entango, Local Voice, and Kintera, which market their sophisticated software and consulting services to charities that want to take advantage of the online fundraising revolution but lack the expertise in-house to do so. For those charities unwilling or unable to make a substantial investment in such a for-profit firm, there are solutions such as Network for Good *(http://www.networkforgood.org)* that provide a low-cost solution to processing online donations, and even subsidize the work they do through foundation and corporate sponsorship. Actually, this particular site used to process donations for free until mid-2003, perhaps influenced by the PipeVine scandal referred to earlier in this book.

New Business Models Attract Partnerships

The technology to handle transactions between charities and the public has improved in sophistication. Software, available for rent or purchase, has made it relatively routine for charities to build Web sites, create attractive online stores, and launch Internet-based marketing programs to bring in substantial revenue. New business models have fostered partnerships with for-profit application service providers (ASPs) that permit charities to focus on their missions of helping people rather than on the business and technology. The availability of inexpensive hardware and software has made it possible for charities to be "do it yourselfers," if they so choose.

> **Charities may choose to set up their online fundraising programs in-house, or they may have an outside application service provider handle all or some aspects of this management task. This chapter explores the costs and benefits of working with such outside contractors to handle online fundraising.**

There are many new for-profit firms (and a few old ones, as well) that are soliciting you and your organizations to help implement an e-philanthropy strategy. In Gary Grobman's book, *The Nonprofit Organization's Guide to E-Commerce,* he writes about the advantages and disadvantages of three options—build, buy, or rent—that charities have in pursuing an e-philanthropy strategy. You can choose building your own site in-house, and there are increasing numbers of resources available that make this option both affordable and accomplishable with a minimum of technical skills. You can buy a custom-designed software package that will be both functional and distinctive. And you can lease an "off the shelf" software suite of services from an ASP that will harness that organization's expertise and experience; handle all of the problems with setup, operation, and maintenance; and take advantage of the economies of scale inherent with having scores of other clients that use a similar software package.

Your choice depends on many factors, including the financial investment you are willing to make; the technical expertise your organization has to design, maintain, repair, and upgrade a site; your comfort level with sharing potentially sensitive information with other organizations; and your willingness to devote the time it takes to make your site successful.

Shaky financial picture for many for-profit partners

Lately, the glamour of the high-tech industry has been tarnished. Few dot-com startup companies have made a profit, and it is difficult for many to conjure up an image of being in the black any time in the near future. Scores of once high-flying dot-coms have gone belly-up. The number of companies that market Internet donation processing and related services to the charitable community, a handful a few years ago, is now about a hundred. Some of these companies are in a precarious financial position, and a few have ceased operations. Some have been bought out. ASPs and charity portals are some of the casualties. We would expect others to follow, as even those in the industry who are optimistic about the future of these companies concede that there is a shakeout going on. Providing additional competition to the startups are traditional fundraising firms that are just beginning to offer e-philanthropy services, and have a well-established client base, a trusted name, and an infrastructure in place.

In the long run, there are likely to be fewer, but stronger, firms offering their e-philanthropy services to an increasing number of charities that will seek these services. And an increasing number of charities will have the capacity to develop and implement their e-philanthropy strategies entirely in-house.

Does this make the "rent" option less attractive? Obviously, it is a major disruption if a charity's application service provider files for bankruptcy and closes its doors without notice. In this turbulent financial climate for dot-coms, charities need to be concerned, if not alarmed. But for those charities that would truly benefit from the "rent" choice, the solution to this dilemma is choosing the right ASP, not avoiding an ASP. Choosing the right ASP involves doing some homework.

In speaking recently with CEOs of ASPs, we got the impression that the industry leaders are not yet profitable, but that most are financially stable. However, the venture capitalists who funded startups arc now much more interested in net revenue and the potential for net revenue compared to their expectations just a few years ago, when market share and the number of customers were more important outcome measurements. Some companies will not survive the current crunch, but many others will. Those that do survive will be the ones that add value to the charities they serve, build a trusting relationship, and achieve the results their clients expect.

Questions to Ask

What should charities do? First, for those who feel that the "rent" decision makes sense, it is much more important to choose the right ASP today than it was only a short time ago. It is now not only "reasonable" to ask tough questions before signing a contract with an ASP, but it is essential. Among questions to ask are:

- How long have they been in business?
- Who are the investors?
- Who are the key staff in leadership positions?
- Do staff have experience working for or leading nonprofit organizations, and thus understand your organization's needs?

- Are their motivations consonant with yours?
- What level of employee turnover is the company experiencing? How many employees does the company have now, and how does this compare to a year ago?
- What job openings are advertised on the company Web site?
- Do these advertisements give evidence for organizational expansion, or that current employees are leaving a sinking lifeboat?
- Who are the current clients of the ASP?
- Are they satisfied with the service?
- Have they noticed anything negative about the service lately or other warning signs of financial problems of the ASP?
- Can the standard contract be modified to suit your organization's special needs and concerns?
- What notice is required before service is terminated for any reason?
- What are the terms and conditions for recovering damages from an ASP when something goes awry?

Is the ASP willing to put the code for your site in escrow in the event of a dissolution? Some companies are willing to accommodate this request, although there may be an additional charge for that service. Having the code in escrow will take the nonprofit a long way if it has to start over from scratch in the unlikely event that the ASP folds unexpectedly.

Patent, license, and other legal issues may make it difficult for an ASP to agree to this, but transporting this code from one environment to another is much more technologically complex than, let's say, changing your organization's Web server.

Charities can be choosy

Our conclusion is that application service providers are an appropriate choice for many charities that want to focus on their core missions rather than suffering the headaches of managing an e-philanthropy operation. Charities need to be more choosy today than they used to be in making their choice of ASP. As more and more ASPs enter the market and compete for your business, we would expect competition to become fierce, and the salespeople to be more and more accommodating to your needs for information. If the marketing staff of the ASP gives you the impression that they are evasive or not completely forthcoming, there are scores of honest, trustworthy, and, at least in the short term, financially stable competitors who will do what it takes to help your charity maximize its potential to harness the power of the Internet to build lasting and lucrative relationships.

Be sensitive to legal and tax issues

The legal and tax issues that arise as a result of these partnerships are unexplored territory, and there may be some gray areas worthy of discussion. First, it is not entirely clear that the value of donations made through some for-profit Web sites is tax-deductible, as is claimed by some of these sites. Second, if purchases are made directly from a charity's Web site, it is possible that the charity may be subject to unrelated business income taxes. Third, if a charity promotes the commercial site in its newsletters and other mailings, it may put its preferential postal rates at risk.

Evaluating ASPs

For those who arc considering participating in one of these partnerships, we offer the following advice, some of which is similar or identical to that we offer for evaluating online auction ASPs:

1. Ask lots of questions. Know exactly what your commitments and responsibilities are with respect to the agreement or contract. Direct your questions not only to the application service provider, but to charities that are already participating.

2. Review the Web site of the ASP from top to bottom. Read the site's FAQ (most legitimate sites have one). Read and feel comfortable with the privacy policy (most legitimate sites have one). Make sure you are comfortable with the merchant list.

3. Don't agree to an unreasonably long-term contract that would prohibit your organization from signing up with another provider if you get a better deal somewhere else, or if you are dissatisfied with the ASP's performance. With the intense competition going on, you may get a better deal from a site in a year or two that might not even exist today.

4. Understand how and when your organization will receive checks.

5. Know what the sponsor expects from your charity. Do they want you to provide them with the e-mail addresses of everyone on your board and membership so they can target unsolicited and annoying promotional messages to your constituency? Just say "no."

6. Know and be comfortable with all of the fees and charges involved in the agreement.

7. Verify that the sponsor provides adequate customer service.

8. Know what your organization's commitment will be with respect to ending the relationship, in the event that this becomes necessary for any reason.

9. Consider the track record/trust factor in your decision. Are you comfortable with the motivations of the founders? Are their members and merchants growing? Are there any records of complaints against them filed with the Better Business Bureau? Are they comfortable answering your questions, or do they make you feel that you are a nuisance wasting their time?

10. Consider who in your organization will authorize the decision on participation. Can it be made by the executive director alone, the executive director in consultation with the board chair, or does a decision need to be made by the board?

Resources

Capaciteria
http://www.capaciteria.org/

This site is one of the more interesting new Web sites that have evolved to help charities sort through the complexities of choosing application service providers to help them with their online fundraising needs. The site is a self-professed "labor of love" by Jonathan Peizer, who launched it in June 2005 as a sabbatical project. At the time of our review in early 2006, the site had links of resources in 101 categories, including *Fund Raising, Grants Management & Philanthropy,* and *Information & Communications Technology.* Each has subcategories. What makes the site unique and valuable is that it not only gives you information about the resource and a link to it, but also provides the opportunity for viewers to rate the value of the site on a scale of 1-5 and submit a site review. Very few reviews were available on the site, but this would be expected since it is a relatively new site. We would anticipate that as more folks find out about Capaciteria, it will have more peer-reviewed content and become an even more indispensable resource to nonprofit organizations.

Entango

http://www.entango.com

For a fee, this for-profit company provides nonprofits with full-service online donation processing and other services. At this site, you can "test-drive" Web-based fundraising models that handle event management, online donations, membership renewals, and e-commerce and get a good feel for what the "rent" option discussed in this chapter and Chapter 12 would look like.

Eric Mercer's How to Choose a Web Hosting Agent

http://www.nonprofits.org/npofaq/16/22.html

This 1998 article still provides lots of sage advice on what issues to consider before choosing an online fundraising application service provider.

Kintera

http://www.kintera.com

Kintera, with more than 15,000 clients, in one of the leading full-service online fundraising for-profit application service providers.

The Nonprofit Matrix

http://www.nonprofitmatrix.com/about.asp

This site is a directory of commercial providers who provide online fundraising services to charities, such as auctions, shopping malls, online communities, online donation processing, events management, and "all-in-one" providers that will handle all of a charity's needs. The site is well-organized by 15 categories of services. Its major drawback is that the commercial providers submit the descriptions themselves, and there is no opportunity for feedback such as is available from other sites, such as Capaciteria (see review on page 116). Where there is interactivity with charities, it is from the ability to share links to resources. You can click on the Library "Resources" for articles about e-philanthropy. Among them is Michael Stein's *Elementary e-Philanthropy* from 1999, which is an oldie, but goodie.

Putnam Barber's Resources for Fundraising Online

http://www.nonprofits.org/npofaq/misc/990804olfr.html

This site is an alphabetical listing of resources, many of which are ASPs, that includes links and a short description. The organizations have not been independently evaluated, but this is a useful place to begin exploring what services are offered, and which organizations are providing services.

The Philanthropy Journal home page at:http://www.philanthropyjournal.com.
Reprinted with permission.   See a review of this Web site on page 127.

Chapter 9

Online Networking and Research

There are three easy ways you can use the Internet to improve your expertise as a fundraiser. First, you can use it as a networking tool to "meet" peers through electronic mailing lists and newsgroups. Second, you can use the 'Net as a "library" to learn fundraising skills and develop creative ideas through the many articles and online materials, books, and courses on the topic. Third, you can use it as a "newsstand," and keep up with your field by visiting or subscribing to Web sites of philanthropy publications.

Mailing Lists

Suppose you are clamoring for a quick, unbiased evaluation of fundraising software from those who have actually used it rather than those who developed it or market it. Or you need to find out what luck your colleagues around the world are having with direct solicitation of prospects by e-mail. Or perhaps you are seeking answers to, or opinions about, a myriad of other real-life dilemmas of a seasoned professional in the field.

You need practical advice, and you need it now, if not yesterday.

Increasingly, professionals in nonprofit organizations are turning to the Internet for information, and Internet mailing list postings are becoming the tool of choice to connect those who have information and are willing to share it with those who need it. In one such forum recently, Gary Grant exchanged samples of Powerpoint presentations for educating board members about fundraising. The individual needing a model had samples just minutes after posting her request. And about 20 other people jumped at the opportunity to get a copy themselves and to see how their colleagues presented such information. What makes these communication transactions even more attractive is that they are fast and free.

Mailing list subscriptions a click away

In our 1998 book *The Non-Profit Internet Handbook,* we wrote that the Internet is "like having your own private library, entertainment center, news and clipping service, professional conference, private club, and nightly gala soirée." Internet mailing lists often achieve each of these objectives. Once you subscribe, usually by sending a simple e-mail with the word "subscribe," your e-mail address, and real name, you receive the "mail," a series of e-mail messages that subscribers to the list send that get broadcast to every subscriber on the list. These e-mails arrive in your Internet mailbox either individually as each message is posted, or in a daily digest consisting of a single message that contains all of the posts for that day.

> **The Internet provides a convenient way to network with other online fundraisers, and find out about new developments affecting online fundraising. Among the resources available online are:**
>
> - **electronic newsletters**
> - **online philanthropic news sources**
> - **electronic mailing lists**
> - **online courses**
> - **online publications and online sources to purchase conventional publications**

Some of these mailing lists are "moderated"—that is, each message is reviewed by a list supervisor for appropriateness before it is posted to all members of the list. Others are unmoderated, and members self-police the list by punishing those who transgress the list's netiquette by sending flame messages—personal e-mails disparaging the violators. Similarly, some are open to the public and others require approval to join.

There has been a veritable explosion in the number and quality of these lists recently. Newly developed software, corporate sponsorship, and an explosion of Internet advertising have increased the ease by which anyone, regardless of technical expertise or budget, can create a quality mailing list.

You can find more than 30 public mailing lists frequented by nonprofit board members and staff simply by pointing your Web browser to: *http://charitychannel.com/forums/.* There is a modest subscriber fee for these mailing lists, and you can sample them before paying the subscription fee, because payment is by the honor system. To subscribe, send an e-mail with no message to: (insert name of the list)-subscribe-request@CharityChannel.com. For example, to subscribe to the list on annual funds, send a blank e-mail to: ANNUAL_FUND-SUBSCRIBE-REQUEST@CharityChannel.com. You can also subscribe by filling out an online form at: *http://charitychannel.com/forums/#* (click on the list you want to join).

Among the popular lists for fundraisers are (in alphabetical order) with the address to subscribe are:

ALUMNI-L (for alumni relations discussions)
Fill out the online form at: http://ws1.case.org/cgi-bin/wa.exe?SUBED1=alumni-l&A=1

Annual_Fund (annual fund development)
To subscribe: Send a blank e-mail to ANNUAL_FUND-SUBSCRIBE-REQUEST@CharityChannel.com

ARNOVA-L (nonprofit organizations and voluntary action)
To subscribe, visit: *http://www.arnova.org/listserv.php*

E-Philanthropy (online fundraising)
To Subscribe: Send a blank e-mail to E-PHILANTHROPY-SUBSCRIBE-REQUEST@CharityChannel.com

Fundclass (general fundraising)
To subscribe, fill out the online form at: *http://www.fundraisersoftware.com/library/fundclass/fundclass-subscribe.html*

Fundraising (general fundraising)
To subscribe, see: *http://www.egroups.com/subscribe.cgi/fundraising* and follow the subscription instructions.

FundList (general fundraising)
To subscribe, send an e-mail to: listproc@listproc.hcf.jhu.edu with the message in the body: subscribe FundList <firstname lastname> and follow the instructions for joining Yahoo! lists.

GRANTS (general grants)
To subscribe: Send a blank e-mail to GRANTS-SUBSCRIBE-REQUEST@CharityChannel.com.

Nonprofit (general nonprofit organization issues)

To subscribe, fill out the form at: *http://www.rain.org/mailman/listinfo/nonprofit*

Message Boards

A similar method of networking is the message board. Especially attractive to those who don't want their mailbox inundated with discussions, message boards allow the fundraiser to go to a Web site to read and post messages, respond to each other, and share files and pictures only when they choose to participate. A message board forum is often supplemented with e-mail. For example, many can be set to send you an e-mail when someone responds specifically to a question you posted.

Yahoo! Groups feature many such forums, such as ShelterFundraising—a forum specific to fundraisers of animal shelters and rescues (see http://groups.yahoo.com/group/ShelterFundraising/).

Another popular forum resource is Delphi Forums (http://forums.delphiforums.com/). Services like these make it easy to set up your own professional forum.

"Netiquette" is similar for both mailing lists and message boards. Before diving into uncharted, potentially treacherous waters, we advise both "newbies" and experienced users alike to consider the following advice:

1. "Lurk" (that is, spend some time reading postings on a mailing list or message board for a while before submitting a post) to get a feel for what types of messages are appropriate, and the "culture" of the list.

2. Read the FAQ (frequently asked questions) file, which is periodically posted as a message on many lists so the list does not get clogged up with the same queries over and over.

3. Save the subscribing information that is sent to you when you join a list. This will be useful when you need to unsubscribe.

4. Consider unsubscribing from very active lists if you are away from your computer for an extended period of time, such as when you are on vacation, particularly if you do not receive your postings in daily digests. Keep in mind that most Internet Service Providers provide limited mailbox storage space, and you can lose all of your e-mail permanently if your allotment of memory is exceeded.

5. Don't "flame" other members. You may not know when the person flamed will be your next boss. Flaming contests sometimes get out of control and can be very irritating to others on the list. They usually do nothing to further the purposes of the list, which are to share information and network. Be respectful of the opinions of others. Our advice has been when someone flames you, even if their attack was unprovoked, simply ignore him or her.

6. Keep the message short and on topic. You should think twice before posting a message that you judge not to be of direct interest to the list. If you must post something that is off topic, indicate this in the subject line. Keeping your message short and concise is wise, because most people won't read a message for too long. Let your ideas come out over time in the discussion rather than writing a treatise.

7. Don't post commercial messages or advertisements. Information about a new product or service is sometimes acceptable (check the FAQ file if you are not sure), but most "selling" on mailing lists is verboten.

8. Don't post anything you would be uncomfortable with seeing on the front page of your daily newspaper. There are cases when such publication has actually occurred.

9. Contribute to the list; don't just benefit from it. The valuable information you receive from your posted query comes from someone who cares enough to do some work, perhaps even some research, to share information with you. You should feel some responsibility to assist others if you can, provided you have something worthy to offer to them.

10. Don't post to the entire list when a private e-mail message would be more appropriate.

11. Use sarcasm and humor sparingly. They don't translate well in e-mail communication, and an offhand comment might be taken very seriously by one or more readers.

12. Don't disparage your organization or its board or staff in your messages. They may well be subscribers to the list, or know someone who is.

13. Don't post copyrighted material in your messages without permission from the creator of the material. This is not simply courtesy; it is a legal issue, as well.

14. Make sure that you post messages to the list rather than to the administrative address and vice versa. The e-mail address to subscribe, unsubscribe, or obtain information about a list is different from the address to which you send messages intended for all members of the list.

15. Your responses to posts should be more than "I agree" or "thank you for responding." Try to make your post add something to the discussion, or don't post it at all.

16. Keep appropriate confidentiality in your posting with respect to your organization, its board, staff, and clients.

Electronic Newsletters

You can have news about the sector delivered free to your e-mail inbox by subscribing to electronic newsletters. In contrast to mailing lists, these are e-mails sent to subscribers every week or two that subscribers don't post to with comments for other subscribers to see, i.e., the content is created by the publisher rather than subscribers.

The following is how to subscribe to four valuable, free electronic newsletters:

Philanthropy News Digest (weekly general philanthropy news)
To subscribe: fill out an online form at: *http://fdncenter.org/pnd/*

PNN Online (twice weekly general philanthropy news)
To subscribe: fill out an online form at: *http://wind.he.net/~pnnonl/ newsalerts.php*

Rich Tips (twice monthly general nonprofit management)
To subscribe: send an e-mail with the words "Subscribe Rich Tips" in the subject line to nicolle@richardmale.com

TechSoup's *By the Cup* (weekly nonprofit technology)
To subscribe: fill out an online form at: *http://www.techsoup.org/*

Charity Channel offers 14 electronic newsletters for a token membership fee. For more information, point your browser to: *http://charitychannel.com/enewsletters/*

News About the Nonprofit Sector

Fundraising is a time-consuming occupation. It is important to keep up with news in philanthropy, the latest developments in the field, and the latest laws, regulations, and ethics requirements that apply to fundraisers. The cost of subscribing to professional journals and newspapers is not always a part of a fundraiser's budget, and when it is, the funds are often limited. The Internet offers a terrific opportunity to obtain current news about the sector that is usually free or low cost, convenient, and searchable.

One use of the Internet is to help keep abreast of philanthropic news stories. If your organization primarily serves a local community, then you may want to focus on stories about philanthropists in your community. If your organization is national or global, then you might want to follow stories specifically related to your mission. In doing so, you may gain an opportunity to find or build a connection between your organization and the donor giving elsewhere. Philanthropists tend to be involved with more than one organization, especially over time. The donor who established a new athletic facility for children in your community might also be interested in getting to know your program for at-risk teens.

Following philanthropic stories can be done through several sources. You can review publications specific to fundraising, such as the *Chronicle of Philanthropy (http://philanthropy.com/)*. Your Association of Fundraising Professionals (AFP) *(http://www.afpnet.org/)* chapter site provides stories. To search the general media, you might try the very practical Google News Alerts *(http://www.google.com/ newsalerts)*, which allows you to enter a search term and receive daily e-mails linking to stories from many different outlets.

Other sites to explore for philanthropic news include:

Nonprofit Times Online *(http://www.nptimes.com/)*
Philanthropy Journal Online *(http://philanthropyjournal.org/)*

Resources

About.com Nonprofit Mailing List
http://NONPROFIT.about.com/gi/pages/mmail.htm

Visit the above URL to subscribe to a mailing list with news about the nonprofit sector.

Charity Channel
http://charitychannel.com/forums

You can read descriptions, subscribe, unsubscribe, and view archives of 33 free, public electronic mailing lists of interest to nonprofits. There is a modest annual

$24 fee to join Charity Channel. You can also subscribe to one of 14 electronic newsletters on nonprofit topics at: *http://charitychannel.com/enewsletters/*

The Chronicle of Philanthropy
http://www.philanthropy.com

The site provides highlights from this publication, which is the trade journal for America's charitable community. The tabloid-format biweekly is the number one source for charity leaders, fundraisers, and grant makers, and the Web site provides more than just a taste of what its subscribers receive in snail mail every two weeks. The site is updated every other week at 9 a.m. on the Monday before the issue date, and job announcements are updated on the Monday following that. You can sign up for a free weekly e-mail update of news and new features of the site, plus breaking news when it occurs. The principal categories of this site are gifts and grants, fundraising, managing nonprofit groups, and technology. Each of these headings is further divided by a news summary, workshops and seminars, and deadlines. Also on the site are front-page news stories, a news summary, conferences, Internet resources, products and services, and jobs. Most of the articles consist of one-sentence summaries but are still useful, particularly if you don't have the $72 in your budget to subscribe to the print publication for a year. The "Jobs" button transports you to a searchable database of hundreds of positions available. In some respects, this searchability makes the Internet version of the *Chronicle* more useful than the conventional version. There is also a handy directory of "Products and Services." If you are a subscriber, you will have access to a handy, searchable database of archived issues.

Michael Gilbert's Nonprofit Online News
http://gilbert.forms.soceco.org/50/

This free online newsletter is available at the Web site, or by a weekly e-mail. It is a publication of the Gilbert Center, founded by Michael Gilbert, a well-known private nonprofit consultant who also established the Online Fundraising mailing list. The lively, chatty news articles in this e-zine are spiced with hyperlinks that often lead to interesting surprises of interest to those who follow nonprofit technology issues. Visit the above URL to subscribe to this free, weekly electronic newsletter.

The Nonprofit Times
http://www.nptimes.com

This is the online version of the monthly tabloid newspaper. It has full-text articles from the latest issue, as well as classified advertisements. The Resource

Directory accessible from the home page links to a database of vendors, consultants, and other professionals who serve the nonprofit community.

Philanthropy News Network
http://www.pnnonline.org

This site is a spinoff of the *Philanthropy Journal*, a Raleigh, N.C.-based newspaper for the nonprofit sector that discontinued its print publication in March 2000. Full-text articles on issues of interest to nonprofits, and generous coverage of technology issues, are available at this site's home page. A free e-mail with capsule summaries of articles in the current issue is available for subscription. The entire site is searchable, and current articles are categorized by a number of topics, including "General Fundraising."

Philanthropy Journal
http://www.philanthropyjournal.com

This online news site is a service of the A. J. Fletcher Foundation. Updated daily, it includes news, information and opinion about charitable giving, fundraising and management.

Pulse
http://www.allianceonline.org/publications/Pulse/pulse_0106.pul

Pulse, a free, bimonthly e-newsletter for the nonprofit management community published by the Alliance for Nonprofit Management *(http://www.allianceonline.org)*.

Rick Christ's Nonprofit Internet Resources
http://www.rickchrist.com

Edited by Rick Christ, a private nonprofit technology and marketing consultant, this site offers useful information on e-mail for fundraising and marketing. More than 100 articles are archived for searching, including a comprehensive research paper on Internet Fundraising. You can subscribe to the monthly, free *e-fund News* electronic newsletter here.

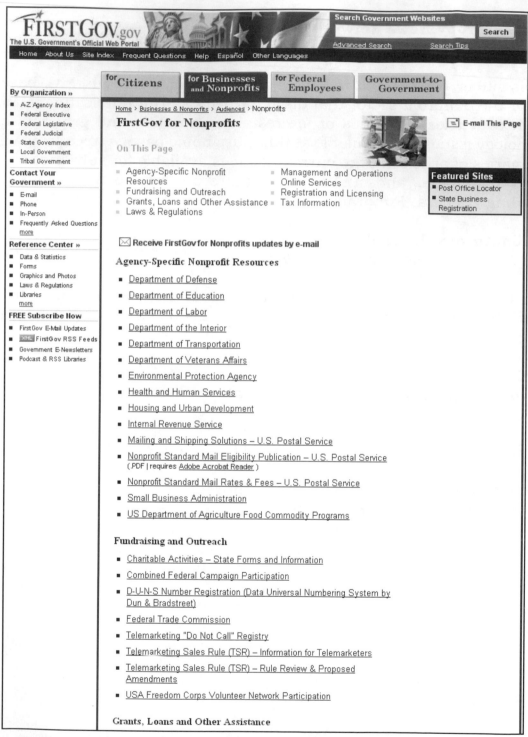

The FirstGov home page (excerpt) at: http://www.firstgov.gov. Reprinted with permission. See a review of this Web site on page 80.

White Hat Communications

Chapter 10

Building an Online Community to Enhance Fundraising

It is not likely that your organization will be able to compete with America Online and attract tens of millions of members who will spend hours and hours each week visiting your site. But AOL and some of the most familiar names on the Internet, from eBay to Yahoo!, to Lycos, to HandsNet, have made their mark by creating and maintaining online communities of loyal Web site visitors. Loyal visitors build relationships. Whether it is through donations, opportunities to volunteer or participate in advocacy efforts, product purchases, or simply feedback, nonprofit organizations thrive on relationships with individuals. There is perhaps no better strategy for building relationships on the Internet than establishing an online community.

What is an Online Community

An online community is any Web site that attracts people who have something in common and allows them to contribute to content or discussions on the site. The types of services that are typically available are real time chat, forums or message boards, member directories, instant messaging (such as AOL's "buddy" program), as well as job/career information, shopping, and news and information. What members of the site have in common can be anything: their age, their social status, their profession, their religion, their politics, their health concerns, or interest in a particular public policy issue.

What distinguishes online communities from other Web sites is that much of the content is contributed by visitors. This content may be moderated by the Web site host, although in many cases it is not.

E-philanthropy and online communities

Online communities and e-philanthropy create a natural marriage. Visitors to online communities tend to be loyal, returning again and again, often night after night. What attracts them is the opportunity to interact with people like themselves. The experience is enhanced when technology permits this interaction to occur in real time. Today, a visitor may come to the site without a specific goal just to look around and see what topics are being discussed or what information is there. They can then become more interested in the organization and its successes and ultimately be willing to financially support the organization. Some day (and that day may be this year or next), these visitors may be clicking on the "donate here" icon.

How to Create an Online Community

Those online communities that are successful are the ones that have found a way to reach a critical mass of participants.

We noticed a problem with Microsoft Network's nonprofit forums when we were reviewing this site for our 1998 book, *The Non-Profit Internet Handbook*. The technical platform was first class. But virtually all of the messages came from one person, who obviously was handpicked by Microsoft to generate content.

> **Online communities facilitate fundraising by building loyal traffic to your organization's Web site. They require constant maintenance, as well as raise issues of privacy. A Code of Conduct is essential.**

We recommend that you find at least a dozen people who are committed to the online community concept, and have them all agree to actively participate. Obviously, no one will come back to a chat room that doesn't have anyone in it, or has people making small talk. Publicity must be focused and fierce! People will need a good reason to visit and register. Make it worth their while. Advertise on electronic mailing lists and in your newsletters. Send e-mail and snail mail to your donors, and make sure all organization staff join and participate. Once up and running, online forums can develop a life of their own and require less "push" to keep them going strong.

Suppose, for example, that your organization provides care for abandoned dogs. An online community for dog owners could be sponsored at your site. You would develop discussion forums for dog owners, encouraging the community of dog owners in your area to share tips with each other, advising on the best vets in the area, or even encouraging them to set up mutual dog sitting or dog walking activities. A forum might be dedicated to the organization's volunteers. Staff could also participate in the forums.

In part, this may be a service to the community consistent with your mission and also a service to those who have adopted pets. But it's also a way to maintain a loyal following—people who may not consider you among their regular charities, but who might, if involved like this, give from time to time.

Active participation builds community

Linda Grobman, Gary Grobman's wife, established an online community for social workers and social work students in 1997 that is still going strong. To meet the needs of her community (which also keeps people coming back), she used to hold periodic, moderated chats on the same evening each week (with a devoted community member volunteering as host), and continues to moderate a message board, provides discounts for products in the site's store, and, far and away the best marketing tool for promoting site visits, posts new job listings that not only provide a free service to job seekers but generate substantial income from job posters. She advertises the site in publications subscribed to by her target market, such as the monthly tabloid of the National Association of Social Workers. But the primary source of the site's continued growth is her own active participation in the social work community-at-large—both online and off-line.

Challenges of Online Communities

- Creating and maintaining an online community requires substantial time and ongoing effort.

- Some visitors post inappropriately, such as putting slanderous or libelous messages on the message board, posting commercial messages, violating confidentiality, or infringing on a copyright.

- Some words used in real time posting may be offensive, requiring the use of filtering software. It is difficult to choose which words to censor.

- Online communities need an effective Code of Conduct.

Even when the online community is free, almost every one requires members to register, select a user name, and select a password. Doing so assures that the site has at least a minimum of control over denying access to those who consistently violate its Code of Conduct. There are also marketing reasons to have a password-protected site, in that when visitors register, they can provide useful demographic information.

One benefit of these access restrictions is the ability to enforce the rules of the online community.

Legal Issues

Establishing an online community exposes the organization to legal liability in a number of areas that are unsettled, chiefly because of the fact that many technology issues are new and haven't been tested in the courts. It is not unusual for landmark cases to take 10 years before they are resolved by the U.S. Supreme Court, and commercial use of the Internet is barely that old. In 1996, the Congress enacted *The Communications Decency Act,* which has a provision that under certain conditions, a service provider is not the "publisher" when a user posts material that is considered defamatory on an interactive Web site. This provision was upheld in U.S. District Court in a case decided in 1998 involving America Online and political columnist Matt Drudge.

Codes of conduct

A Code of Conduct is a necessity, as is a privacy statement (see Chapter 13).

The Code should include what behaviors are not permitted by site users, such as flaming; obscene, sexist, anti-Semitic, or racist postings; the posting of copyrighted material without permission from the copyright owner; the uploading of files, such as software or other materials that are a violation of intellectual property laws; and engaging in fraudulent conduct or harassment of other users.

One concern pointed out by legal experts is that your Web site is accessible globally, and each country has its own laws with respect to what is acceptable content. It is not clear how the courts will enforce the laws of foreign countries with respect to content on your U.S.-based site.

Resources

DraGoNet
http://www.alumniconnections.com/olc/pub/DXU/

This is a good example of a nonprofit (Drexel University of Philadelphia) using a password-protected online community to build relationships with potential donors, in this case, alumni. The site is "rented" from the Bernard C. Harris Publishing Company (see: *http://www.harrisconnect.com/isd/index.html),* which custom-designs online community Web sites for schools and other organizations.

Yale Alumni
http://www.aya.yale.edu/

This is an example of an alumni online community site. Here you can find a password-protected site that includes message boards, alumni directories, career services, information about reunions, pages for each Yale graduating class, publications, and, of course, a link to "Giving to Yale."

**The iGive home page at:http://www.igive.com.
Reprinted with permission. See a review of this
Web site on page 98.**

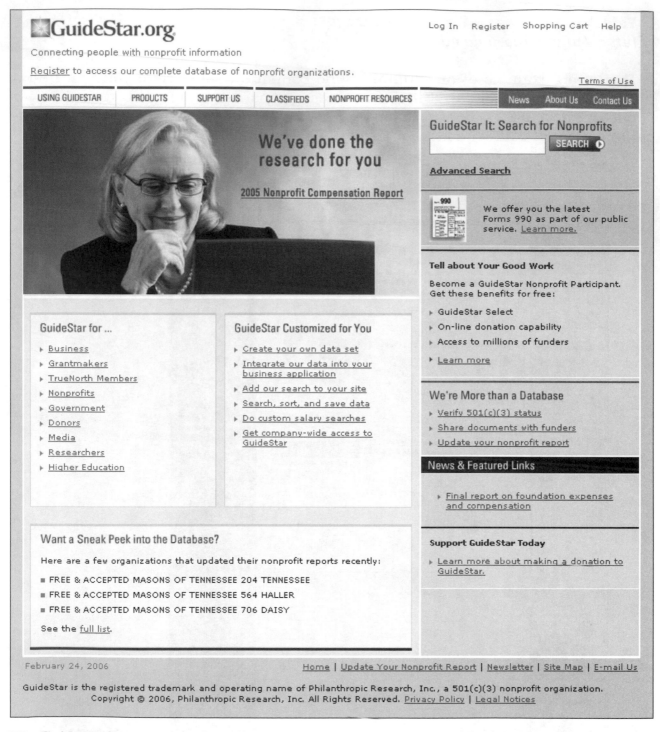

The Guidestar home page at: http://www.guidestar.org. Reprinted with permission. See a review of this Web site on page 140.

Chapter 11

Sites That Help Donors Evaluate Organizations

Savvy for-profit businesses routinely search the Web for useful information about their customers' needs, their competitors, and how customers view their products and services. When Gary Grobman performs his monthly routine search of his own name (with and without his middle initial) on a popular search engine such as google.com or altavista.com, he inevitably finds something of value or interest that is worthy of some follow-up. Some search engines, including Google, now provide automatic notices whenever there is new content that includes a keyword, making such a regular search an anachronism.

Periodically Check Out Your Organization's Reputation

Fundraisers should routinely make the same effort with respect to their organizations. An organization makes a major investment in creating a recognizable brand name that has value with respect to generating donations, volunteers, grants, and friends. The Web is a free resource that enables you to find out how your organization is being perceived by your stakeholders.

If your organization's reputation has been tarnished by a failure to meet published ethical standards of one of several watchdog organizations, this information may be publicly posted. Among such popular sites donors visit for information about charities are Guidestar *(http://www.guidestar.org)*, Charity Navigator *(http://www.charitynavigator.org)*, and the Better Business Bureau's Wise Giving Alliance *(http://www.give.org)*. Today's donors are becoming much more sophisticated and less trusting than their predecessors. They are more likely to demand information about the reputation of the charity, how the donation will be used, and whether their money is accomplishing a specific, measurable outcome, rather than simply writing a check and hoping the organization is worthy. The Web facilitates these donors with several sites that have databases providing information about specific charities, including yours.

Scores of sites have emerged that tailor their content to the needs of philanthropists. It is obvious that the information provided on these sites is of interest to organization fundraisers, as are the random mentions of your organization that can be found on search engines.

We recommend performing searches on your organization's name periodically and seeing how your organization is perceived generally. Equally important is visiting these philanthropy portals and other sites for donors, and making sure that the information portraying your organization is both accurate and positive. And even more important is making sure your organization conducts its business both legally and ethically.

> **Nonprofit organizations should monitor what is being said about them on the Internet by public sources found on search engines, and organizations that evaluate charities.**

The Internet influences philanthropy in ways that fundraisers can't necessarily control, but for which fundraisers must be prepared. One example of this is the increasing use donors are making of charity rankings published online by a variety of organizations seeking to protect donors' interests. Increasingly, donors are availing themselves of charity rankings as a way to evaluate the organizations they consider supporting.

This phenomenon may be a controversy in the making, however. Rankings tend to dramatically simplify the complex questions one must ask to fully and accurately understand the quality and worthiness of a not-for-profit organization.

Limitations of Charity Watchdog Group Data

Most accrediting agencies and other groups charged with judging an organization's quality typically engage in an arduous task of collecting data and analyzing programs in great detail. Such reviews put an organization under a microscope.

Charity watchdog groups, however, look more through a telescope. Often based only on available annual reports and a single piece of data or a simple formula, they apply their rankings. Too often donors read these as though they were fully researched evaluations of a program. For example, a common approach is to base the rankings on the ratio of dollars raised to fundraising expenses. The higher ranked organizations are those that "efficiently" spend the least to raise a dollar.

This information is certainly relevant for donors to know and it is a useful statistic when evaluating an organization. But alone, it may not be helpful in determining an organization's worthiness and can be misleading as a basis for comparison to other organizations. Not-for-profit organizations differ by nature, but under this standard, organizations that depend on many donors giving small average gifts would be automatically ranked lower than organizations that depend on a few donors giving large major gifts. Obviously, such fundraising realities have no bearing on which is better managed. Differences in funding sources don't necessarily have anything to do with the quality of the work done by the organization, nor do they show any kind of fiscal irresponsibility.

Similarly, consider those organizations that seek to educate people about public interest issues. They tend to mail their donors more, because the communication itself is part of achieving its mission. But such an organization would be ranked lower than those that have less need to communicate broadly. Further, organizations that are younger may spend more in their first few years as they build a donor base. Finding donors is more costly than retaining loyal donors. Again, the need to communicate broadly, the youth of an organization, and similar factors will work to lower an organization's rankings without speaking to whether the group is truly worthy of a donor's philanthropy. And yet as a result of the lower ranking, donors will be turned off to giving to them. If your organization is one of these, it will be a major and growing concern for you.

While donors could (and should) look to these rankings with a careful eye, many do not. Fundraisers must therefore include in their Internet fundraising strategy a position statement addressing the questions likely to be raised by donors. The statement should be geared to helping donors appropriately interpret the rankings.

Gather data on your charity's rankings

Fundraisers need to start by gathering data on their rankings with different charity watchdog groups. Don't wait until a donor brings it to your attention. Be at least as Internet savvy as your philanthropic constituency. In addition to finding out your scores with these groups, also record their methodologies if they publish them.

How to Respond to Questions Relating to Ranking Sites

Once you assess how you are being ranked, check the accuracy of your ranking. If you have been ranked lower than you should be, contact the site and offer the corrected data. If they don't follow your request for a review, then you will at least be able to explain to donors that you tried to do so and encourage them to be discerning in their evaluation of the site upon which they are relying. It's fair to ask if anyone is watching the watchdog organizations.

Next, take the time to document other organizations that may be similar to yours or perhaps competing with you. You will need to know more than just your own organization's score, but how you stack up compared to others. Even scores you think are too low may be easier to deal with if they are similar throughout the field.

This is not meant to be hostile to watchdog organizations. They do serve a valuable purpose and in the future will likely correct some of their weaknesses. But until there is more complete data gathering and analysis of organizations, fundraisers will have to have a ready response to the concerns donors may raise. It is important to ensure that the good and useful information is not being misused in judging quality programs in need of support. As a fundraiser, you are in a good position to clarify this for your donors and to help them accomplish what they really want—which is to know that they are giving to a worthy organization that will spend their gift wisely.

Your answer to donors who raise concerns they develop from watchdog sites should:

- Express appreciation that they are trying to ensure they are making a wise gift and investing in the right organization. You don't want to be confrontational with donors or to denigrate the idea of the watchdog groups. Doing so risks insulting donors who obviously placed some value in the resource if they are bringing its result to your attention.

- Respond honestly to questions when your cost to raise a dollar is higher than other organizations. Don't dance around the issue. If it is higher, then explain why that is.

- Address whether major donors or others can restrict their gifts so that 100% of the money goes to the program or cause. If this is the case, they may not worry so much about the total ratios, so long as overall they are still reasonable.

- Consider other ways donors can assure themselves that you are the best place to give support for your particular mission. Help donors judge you in ways that are more accurate if you think your rankings are misleading. Some possibilities include talking with board members or program beneficiaries, or looking at other data on how you manage your revenues and expenses. If there are any other third party evaluations on the quality of your programs, use these to help your donor constituency be confident in your organization.

Anticipate donor questions

You can feel free to incorporate your case for donor trust and faith on your organization's Web site. Anticipating the donors' needs in this regard will help to increase their comfort level with giving. Doing this may help with donors who don't take the time to communicate the concerns they are having and who don't give you the chance to respond to what they find at charity rating sites.

Resources

Charitable Choices
http://www.charitablechoices.org

This site provides 10 criteria necessary for eligibility in the Combined Federal Campaign. These standards are codified in federal regulations published in November 1995, and include reporting requirements, low fundraising and administrative costs, governance standards, honest promotion and use of funds, and a minimum level of 20% of income derived from public support (see: *http://www.charitablechoices.org/cfc_stand.asp*).

Charity Navigator
http://www.charitynavigator.org

Charity Navigator, founded in 2001, is a 501(c)(3) itself. On this site is a free database of financial information about more than 5,000 charities. Charities are rated on their organizational efficiency and their organizational capacity based on the most current IRS 990 annual tax return available. Charities receive a rating from zero to four stars, and can be compared to peer organizations with a click of the mouse. Ratings take into account the location, size, and how a charity functions financially. The site also provides selective salary information for CEOs.

Council of Better Business Bureaus (CBBB) Wise Giving Alliance
http://www.give.org

The National Charities Information Bureau (NCIB) and the Council of Better Business Bureaus' (CBBB) Philanthropic Advisory Service merged in 2001 to form the Better Business Bureau's Wise Giving Alliance. From the home page, click on "Charity Reports" from the menu and find an index of reports compiled on hundreds of charities. Attached to each name is an indication of whether the charity has been evaluated as to whether it is in compliance with 23 voluntary standards relating to public accountability, use of funds, solicitations and informational materials, fundraising practices, and governance. The standards can be found at: *http://www.give.org/standards/cbbbstds.asp*. A nine-part standard that was used by the NCIB, but is no longer operational because of the merger, may be found at: *http://www.give.org/standards/ncibstds.asp*. A typical report is quite comprehensive. In addition to contact information, the report describes the organization's purpose, whether it meets the CBBB standards, chapter and verse as to why one or more of these standards are not met, financial information, number on the board, number of paid staff, methods of fundraising, fundraising costs, sources of funds by category, assets and liabilities, and other financial information.

GuideStar

http://www.guidestar.org

GuideStar is administered by Williamsburg, VA-based Philanthropic Research, Inc., a 501(c)(3), and publishes comprehensive reports about individual American charities. Its purpose is "to bring the actors in the philanthropic and nonprofit communities closer together through the use of information and communication technologies. GuideStar collects and analyzes operating and financial data from the IRS Form 990 and from voluntary submissions from the charities themselves." The database consists of more than 1.5 million reports on individual charities, and the site is colorful, accessible, and well-designed. The basic database can be searched at no charge by any number of parameters, such as name, location, or type of charity, and there are fee-based databases on the site that provide even more information. This is simply the best site on the Internet for finding financial information about charities. Charities can provide their reports and update them online at no charge.

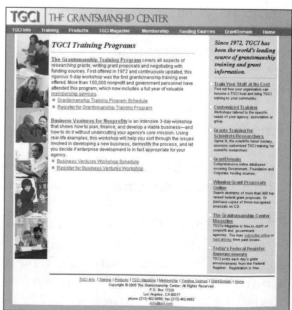

The Grantmanship Center home page at: http://www.tgci.org. Reprinted with permission.

E-Commerce

The main focus of this book is how to use the Internet for fundraising, but we would be remiss if we did not cover a related topic that goes hand-in-hand with online philanthropy—the online marketing of an organization's goods and services. Many of the same techniques and strategies that are effective in generating donations online are equally effective in such marketing. And many of the tools are the same: a Web site, a merchant account to process payments, and a list of e-mail addresses of stakeholders, among others.

Nonprofits that don't take advantage of the natural marriage between e-philanthropy and e-commerce are missing out on an opportunity to generate income. And, after all, that is what fundraising is all about. Few organizations would engage in it if they didn't need revenue, and e-commerce offers opportunities to reduce the need for conventional fundraising.

The term *e-commerce* refers to business that is conducted electronically. It includes the marketing of goods and services, using the Internet to join an organization or subscribe to a publication, and automated customer service.

Technically, using the telephone to place an order also qualifies as e-commerce. So would using your debit card to make a purchase at your local convenience store. This chapter uses a narrower definition, becoming increasingly common in books and articles, to describe business conducted over the Internet. It focuses on how nonprofit organizations can use the Internet to increase membership, market products and services, and respond to customer inquiries and complaints.

Customer service? Marketing? Products? Why does any of this have anything to do with the nonprofit sector? Many of us lose sight of the fact that a nonprofit organization is a form of business. Nonprofits and for-profits have many things in common. Both need capital to launch their operations, both need cash flow to pay their bills in a timely manner, and both need revenues to pay for staff, supplies, utilities, rent, equipment, printing, and other goods and services. Charities typically receive revenues beyond what is gratuitously donated by the public, the business community, or foundations. For example, they sell services. It is typical that a third or more of the revenue from a social service agency comes from user fees. While many agencies charge on a sliding scale based on income, it is not unusual for them to charge a market rate to those who can afford to pay and use the surplus so generated to cross-subsidize those who cannot afford to pay the full costs of services.

The for-profit world has embraced e-commerce, recognizing that it is the future of how business-to-business (B2B) and business-to-consumer (B2C) purchasing will be conducted by millions, if not billions, of participants. As we mentioned in the introduction to this book, the Internet is becoming a convenient way for consumers to make retail purchases. According to the Goldman, Sachs & Co., Nielsen/ NetRatings and Harris Interactive's Holiday eSpending Report, holiday shoppers in the U.S. alone spent $25 billion online through the week ending December 16, 2005. Some of the spending was on goods offered by nonprofits, which recognize that shoppers feel good about sending presents that benefit a favorite charity.

> - **Organizations can use their Web sites not only to solicit donations, but also to sell goods and services.**
> - **There are options to build the site in-house, buy the required software and install it on the organization's site, or "rent" the services from an application service provider.**
> - **E-commerce involves tasks that may not be a part of the traditional charity's repertoire, such as order fulfillment, customer service, returns, shipping and handling, and sales tax collection.**

The business models and strategies used by for-profits can be adapted by nonprofits to generate revenue that will finance the expansion of nonprofit organizational programs and activities. At the very least, these techniques make it a bit easier to raise funds and thus reduce what must be one of the leading causes of stress and burnout among nonprofit executives and staff—the constant battle to raise dollars to balance organizational budgets.

For years, charities have generated income through a variety of programs and activities, such as selling newsletter subscriptions and other publications, collecting fees at conferences and workshops, operating thrift shops, conducting flea markets and running races, renting mailing lists, having auctions, scheduling fundraising dinners, and selling group outings to sporting events or theater performances.

The Web has made all of this easier, at least for many organizations, in two significant ways. First, it has provided organizations with a way to reach almost everyone, and to do this quickly and inexpensively. Using a combination of strategies, such as conventional mail, telephone, and media advertising, along with Web postings, mailing list postings, broadcast e-mail, and Web advertising, an organization can reach its target market and expand its reach. Second, using sophisticated technology, organizations can take advantage of homebound volunteers (at one end of the scale) and pricey, professional "back end" providers (at the other end of the scale) to do much of the work.

As a result of e-mail, the Web, electronic mailing lists, and real-time chat, the velocity of business transactions has made a quantum leap. The Internet has salient advantages over conventional sales marketing, such as—

- Overall marketing and order processing costs are lower using the Web.
- Organizations can reach a global, targeted market virtually instantaneously.
- A Web-based "store" is open 24 hours/day, seven days/week, and always has free parking.
- The playing field is leveled between small organizations and those with many more resources.
- Business transactions can be consummated electronically without the need for expensive labor or intermediaries, such as brokers.
- Internet search engines and directories bring potential customers to organizations without unreasonably expensive marketing efforts.
- Customer service can be almost completely automated.
- "Back office" for-profit organizations with substantial expertise, labor, and sophisticated software will do the necessary work and make it appear to customers that the nonprofit organization is performing the work.

Build, Buy, or Rent

An organization's Web site is the most visible ingredient of its e-commerce strategy. Organizations have three basic choices in deciding which direction to go. Making the choice depends on factors such as—

- The amount of financial investment they are prepared to make
- The amount of staff time they are willing to devote to building, maintaining, and troubleshooting
- Whether they are comfortable with "off the rack" features or want a site that is state-of-the-art and custom-made
- Their comfort level with outside vendors having access to their financial transactions

- Whether they want to have complete control over their Web sites so, for example, they don't have to depend on private companies to update files when they have the time
- Whether they are comfortable with paying an outside firm based on the amount of revenue that is transacted on their sites
- The importance to them of having all visitors stay on their sites rather than being routed to a private vendor who may subject the visitor to advertising that the nonprofit organization cannot control, or may be inconsistent with the organization's values.

Build: Almost all of the tools a nonprofit needs to build a credible e-commerce site can be found using the links at sites such as *http://www.webmasterengine.com/* and *http://www.applytools.com/*. At these sites, you can find shopping carts, security software, domain name services, bank card services, associate programs, auction software, and Web site promotional services. Much of the software can be downloaded for free.

Buy: If an organization is as well-heeled as the Metropolitan Museum of Art *(http://www.metmuseum.org)*, it can afford to buy the very best. From the appearance of this site, one can expect this organization's investment in hiring a private firm to custom-design a Web site will result in financial dividends over the long run. This site was custom-designed by a locally-based outside firm, Icon Nicholson *(http://www.nny.com/nny/)*. Everything about this site is, pardon the pun, state of the art. Icon Nicholson is one of many commercial firms an organization can use if it chooses to "buy" a Web-based, e-commerce solution.

Rent: Application Service Providers (ASPs) are sprouting up and are advertising in the nonprofit national media about the availability of their services. In this context, renting involves purchasing services from a firm that will, for a monthly or annual fee, "rent" nonprofit organizations a customized e-commerce (and donation processing) site based on a template. The pages usually reside on the server of the ASP.

Setting Up an Online Store

If your organization sells products and services, you can enhance these sales by adding a secure online store to your organization's Web site. Before opening your store, think about costs, how you will handle online transactions, customer service issues, receipts and invoices, tax issues, and shipping.

Costs

What will an e-commerce-enabled Web site cost you? Surprisingly, less than you would think in terms of money (but likely more than you think in time). Here are some typical costs.

Web site hosting. Hosting services can be free for nonprofit organizations. A typical charge is $10/month. If you plan to take credit card information over the Internet, make sure that your Web host has the capability of supporting secure forms for this purpose. Secure online store hosting can be found for, perhaps, $30-$40 per month.

Domain Name Registration. This costs up to $35 annually, although there are discounts for pre-payment, and some registrars such as Go Daddy *(http:// www.GoDaddy.com)* and Register.com *(http://www.register.com)* will register a name for $10 or even less.

Software. Web page construction software such as Microsoft's *FrontPage,* which includes templates for professionally designed pages, can be purchased for under $100 from discount software companies. Some software can be downloaded from the Internet for free. The latest versions of standard word processing programs are capable of saving files in HTML format. An HTML page can be constructed entirely by using Windows Notepad. Shopping carts can be free (often including advertising that may be unwanted or inappropriate) or cost thousands of dollars. Many accessories that are great on a Web site, such as counters, "send to a friend" forms, and language translators, are available for free. One emerging development is the availability of "open source" software, free for downloading in many cases, with hundreds of commercial and volunteer developers creating customized add-ons that are geared to the needs of charities. For a primer on open source software, see Appendix B.

Content. Most nonprofit organizations create their own Web site content. It is not unusual to make a purchase or two of graphics or photographs suitable for the Web, but there are many sources that provide these items for free.

Site Maintenance. It takes time to update Web sites and respond to feedback from visitors. Some organizations are large enough to hire full-time Webmasters to design and maintain sites, and some have the executive director or a technically savvy volunteer do this.

Hardware. If you have a remote virtual Web site host, you don't need anything more than your standard office computer and monitor, which you can buy for perhaps $1,000 for an entire system, including CPU with modem, monitor, and color printer.

SSL Certificate. This ensures that the customers' credit cards and other personal information is secure (see page 157)

Marketing. This can be your largest cost. Advertising the site through print publications, postcards, press releases, banner advertising on other sites, and similar strategies can bring more visitors, but can be expensive.

The bottom line is you can spend as little or as much as you want, but it is possible to obtain everything you need to set up an online store on your existing Web site for no cost. If you do not yet have a site (or even a computer), it is possible to buy everything you need for a one-time investment of $1,000, and a monthly payment of under $50.

Handling Online Financial Transactions

Qualifying for merchant status to accept popular credit cards such as Visa, MasterCard, American Express, and Discover is often routine. An organization typically approaches its bank to set up a merchant account. One can find hundreds, if not thousands, of financial institutions willing to establish merchant accounts on the Web. One way to find them is to search under the terms "credit cards" and "merchant accounts."

Startup fees, account maintenance fees, per transaction fees, and the bank's percentage of sales fee for processing each transaction varies by financial institution and may be negotiable.

Organizations will also need a system for transmitting the information about the transaction to the financial institution for processing—typically a terminal sold or leased by the financial institution—or computer software. The financial institution, within a few business days, credits the organization's account for the amount of the sale after deducting transaction charges. The card number, expiration date, and sales information is entered into the terminal or software (or transmitted through a real-time process, using an online ordering system), and the system verifies that the card is bona fide and the purchaser has not exceeded his or her credit limit. There is some paperwork involved, and occasionally a purchaser will challenge a charge, which can result in a loss of time and revenue, even if the charge is legitimate. On the other hand, entrepreneurial nonprofit organizations may lose out on revenue opportunities unless they satisfy the expectations of their customers by offering online credit card purchases.

An alternative to setting up a merchant account for credit cards is to utilize the services of a third-party payment processor that will accept credit cards for you using a secure, online platform. One such popular provider, PayPal *(https://www.paypal.com),* not only provides this service but also gives access to tools that you can use to build your online store, such as shopping carts, invoices, and shipping/tracking management services. From the home page, click on "Merchant Tools" for details about these services. There are no setup fees to establish an account as a merchant. PayPal charges a fee of from 1.9% to 2.9% (depending on sales volume) plus 30 cents per transaction. There are additional fees for foreign currency transactions. More than 80 million individuals (and perhaps one out of every three online shoppers, according to company representatives) have PayPal accounts. The company was purchased by eBay in 2002 and is quickly becoming the standard for making and receiving online payments.

In June 2005, PayPal established a new system, Website Payments Pro, to accept credit cards directly on your site without having a merchant account (see page 105 for more details).

Customer Service

Depending on what products and services are offered, many of the issues relating to customer service will be the same for a nonprofit as for a for-profit organization. Organizations will need to have policies for, and routines for, processing returns, exchanges, refunds, and shipping.

One obvious disadvantage of shopping over the Internet is that shoppers cannot touch and feel the product, or try it on or try it out. People are more willing to make purchases over the Internet when they feel that they can return the products if they are not completely satisfied. A refunds and returns policy should be posted on your site, and it should be a more liberal policy than one would expect to find at the local mall. This is good business practice; nonprofits certainly don't want to alienate a customer who is also a donor or potential donor. Among the issues that should be addressed are:

1. Will refunds be given in cash or credit for a future purchase?
2. How much time is permitted to elapse before returns will not be accepted?
3. Can returns be made unconditionally, or only for defective products?
4. Is there a restocking fee?
5. Must the product be returned in salable condition in the original packaging?
6. Will shipping and handling also be refunded, or only the product purchase price?

7. Will the organization pay for shipping back returns?
8. Will certain products not be returnable (such as publications, electronics, or jewelry)?

Receipts and Invoices

Products should be shipped with a receipt if pre-paid, or an invoice if payment is due. If they were not prepaid, the invoice should state the terms of payment, such as when the bill is due, and the percentage added to the bill per month for any outstanding balance. The receipt should include the name of the purchaser, the name of the organization, the description of the product(s), the price of each purchase, and the amount of tax, shipping, and handling. Generic accounting software such as Quickbooks, Quicken, MYOB Accounting, or Peachtree provides forms for standard invoices and receipts.

Collecting Taxes

Only the states of Alaska, Delaware, Montana, New Hampshire, and Oregon do not have a state sales and use tax. The sales tax applies to sales made within a state to a purchaser from that same state. The use tax applies to sales of products bought in one state and taken into another. The use tax is intended to be paid by the purchaser and goes to the purchaser's state treasury, although this requirement is rarely, if ever, enforced. Generally, organizations are obligated to collect sales and use taxes on sales they make to customers within their own states.

In November 2004, the Congress extended its moratorium against Internet sales taxes for an additional three years. Sales taxes still must be collected for intrastate purchases in states with sales taxes, although enforcement of this requirement is spotty. Even if an organization is tax exempt, most states still require nonprofit organizations to collect sales taxes on sales they make to customers within the state.

Typically, states require organizations to obtain a sales tax license, and to transmit the collected taxes to the state using a provided form. It is advisable to check with a reputable local business organization, such as the Chamber of Commerce, to find out what the requirements are for collecting and transmitting state sales taxes in a particular state before engaging in the sale of goods and services there.

Shipping and Handling

Organizations need to decide how much they will charge for shipping and handling and display that information prominently on the site. Some shopping cart software provides for letting the customer decide how the product is to be shipped—

automatically adjusting the amount for shipping and handling (such as by using a database provided by UPS or other shippers), based on how much the organization wants to add over the actual cost. They can charge a flat fee for shipping, charge by weight, charge by the number of products ordered, or provide for free shipping if the order exceeds a certain amount. Organizations should also consider policies with respect to out-of-country sales, which raise issues with respect to payment, shipping, and customs duties.

Affiliate Marketing

New business models have emerged that permit nonprofit organizations to take advantage of technology and raise funds that would not have come their way otherwise. Even if your organization does not sell products or services of its own, you can generate revenue by marketing products and services of others through "affiliate" or "associate" programs.

The "affiliate" model was pioneered by Amazon.com. The Seattle-based company simply announced to the world that by placing specially coded links on your Web site, you can earn a commission on purchases of books, CDs, DVDs, videos, electronics, software, video games, toys, or home improvement items that are generated by those links.

Joining the Amazon Associates program involves visiting the Amazon.com site, clicking on the "Join Associates" link at the bottom of the home page, electronically submitting a form provided on the site (after reading and agreeing to the operating agreement), and using tools provided on the site to set up your links to Amazon.com and promote products. Each link has your Associate ID code embedded in it, so when someone buys something from Amazon.com through a link on your site, your organization gets a commission, which is paid quarterly by Amazon.com.

As of 2006, more than 1,000,000 Web sites have become Amazon.com associates. For nonprofits and for-profits alike, this simple, yet revolutionary, business model is generating valuable revenue without the need for any investment or exposure to risk.

Similarly, affiliate programs exist for many other online retailers and online services. Your organization can become an affiliate of eBay, Buy.com, allPosters.com, or CareerBuilder.com, for example. Typically, if a site offers an affiliate program, there will be a link for it somewhere near the bottom of the page, leading to an explanation of how to join and how the program works.

When considering joining an affiliate marketing program, think about how the site you will be affiliating with fits with your organization's mission, as well as how you will incorporate the affiliate program into your own site. For example, if you are joining an affiliate program of an online bookstore (such as Amazon.com), will you place reviews and links to carefully selected books that are in line with your mission, or will you set up a complete store where your site's visitors can buy anything that is available in the affiliated store, encouraging your visitors to do all their shopping through your site, as a way of supporting your organization? Each of these approaches has its pros and cons.

Let's say your organization is an animal shelter. Using the first approach, you can create links to (and perhaps reviews of) books on animal care. This will keep the focus on your mission and promote products that your site's visitors are likely to be interested in. You can target these links to the visitor's interests, so a person who is reading an article about German shepherds will see a link on that page to a book on German shepherds. The conversion rate (from seeing the link to clicking on it to purchasing the item) on such links will be higher than that for random links that are unrelated to your site's content. You will need to monitor the links to make sure that they are up-to-date and the items are still available for purchase.

Using the second approach, you can build a store on your site using an automated data feed (if one is provided), and then "educate" your visitors to "support this site" by shopping there. If your visitors get in the habit of going through your site to make their purchases, you can do well with this method. They may buy animal care books, or they may buy office products, or both—either way, you will earn the commission. However, keep in mind that you do not have complete control over the items that are shown through the data feed, and some items may not be in keeping with the mission or character of your organization.

Advertising

Another way you can generate revenue from your organization's Web site is to allow advertisements to be placed on it. The quickest and easiest way to earn money through advertising is to join Google Adsense (or one of its competitors, such as Yahoo! Publisher Network). Once you join, you will be able to log in to Google's Adsense site and generate HTML code to put on your site. Then ads will begin to appear on your site that correspond with key words in the content of your site. Google will send you a monthly check for a portion of the advertising revenue from these ads.

One downside to this is that you do not have complete control over the content of the ads that appear on your site. You can filter the ads to a certain extent, but it will take some staff or volunteer time to monitor the ads to make sure they are appropriate.

Instead of or in addition to this approach, your organization may decide to sell classified and/or banner advertising directly on your site. You will need to develop a policy stating what types of ads you will accept, your advertising rates, and so forth. And you will need to develop a "media kit" telling advertisers the benefits to them of advertising on your site, the procedure for placing an ad, and how to make payment. If your site is a popular one that is getting a significant amount of traffic in your niche, this can be an excellent way to use your site to generate revenue.

Resources

Electronic Funds Corporation
http://www.achnetwork.com

This commercial site provides a variety of online electronic funds transfer services.

How Affiliate Programs Work
http://www.howstuffworks.com/affiliate-program.htm

This tutorial takes you through what you need to know to understand what affiliate programs are, how they work, who they are for, and how you can use them to generate funds for your organization.

OS Commerce
http://www.oscommerce.com/solutions/oscommerce

At this site, you can download the popular open source (this means no charge to you) OS Commerce e-commerce software, which provides a popular and easy-to-use online store and catalog. You can view online demonstrations of the software here, as well, and find links to organizations that use it.

PayPal
http://www.paypal.com

PayPal, purchased by eBay in 2002, now has 100 million accounts in 55 countries. In 2005, it processed $27 billion in online payment transfers. They must be doing something right. PayPal offers a variety of payment processing tools and services. For a very competitive fee, organizations can sign up for accounts that will permit them to accept credit card payments on their Web sites, by telephone by fax or in person, and process everything online using Paypal's "virtual terminal" service.

TuCows
http://www.tucows.com

TuCows is another portal for obtaining freeware, shareware, and commercial versions of software, including those with e-commerce applications. It boasts of having more than 40,000 software titles available, all tested, reviewed, and rated by staff. The site is searchable by type of software you are looking for and the platform used by your computer. Our January 2006 search on the term "e-commerce" yielded more than 80 matches for products ranging in cost from free to $1,500.

VeriSign Internet Trust Services
http://www.verisign.com

This firm is the most-recognized and trusted brand name in Web site certification authentication. The company's software supports encryption of customer data, and assures visitors that you are who you say you are, so that they will know that the credit card information they transmit to you over the Internet will be safe and secure. VeriSign's Secure Site Services are backed by the NetSure Protection Plan, an extended warranty program against economic loss resulting from the theft, corruption, impersonation, or loss of use of certificate, underwritten by Lloyd's of London. For a free guide to Internet security, click on *Securing Your Web Site for Business* from the home page, which refers you to an online form rather than the publication itself. The $598 no-frills service includes up to $100,000 of insurance coverage and authority to display the VeriSign Secure Site seal.

Webmonkey
http://www.webmonkey.com

This site has almost everything you will ever need to build, maintain, and market your Web site, with an online "how-to" library—suitable for beginners through experts. On our latest visit in January 2006, there was a free eleven-minute podcast available on video blogging. One useful resource is a 6-chapter tutorial on e-commerce (see: *http://hotwired.lycos.com/webmonkey/e-business/building/tutorials/tutorial3.html*). Not sure how to integrate animation, video, MP3 files, and graphics on your site? Articles and tutorials walk you through the process. Whether it's learning the basics of HTML or learning about how to handle fonts, creating tables or frames, this is the place to gather basic information on Web site design and more.

Chapter 13

Miscellaneous Issues

Fundraising on the Internet involves resolving a lot of legal, technical, and ethical issues. In this chapter, we look at several important issues: regulation of online fundraising, privacy, security, and copyright.

Privacy

Despite a global reputation for having an entrepreneurial spirit, our culture in North America also is one that fosters a strong and vibrant voluntary sector, compared to our friends in Europe, Africa, and Asia. As a people, we also value our privacy.

The advance of technology has placed privacy issues front and center on the public policy agenda. Nonprofit organizations are using the Internet to sell goods and services and seek donations. This involves the exchange of credit card information and other data, such as private telephone numbers and addresses, and standard demographic data.

Organizational memberships are solicited online, and the data collected via electronic forms can often be aggregated in databases that are easily shared. Organizations are being asked to collect more and more data to share with funders to justify the value of grants and donations. It is not unusual for charities to be approached by political campaigns, telemarketers, and direct mail solicitors offering to buy organizational mailing lists for a lucrative fee.

Consumers are wary about sharing personal information on the Web, even with trusted organizations. They should be; information shared with a nonprofit organization with which they have a relationship could be inappropriately shared with another organization and be subject to abuse. It is not unusual for savvy consumers with privacy concerns to look on a Web site for the organization's privacy policy, and many sophisticated providers of Web content place their privacy policy on the site in a prominent place.

One feature of the Internet that has contributed to fears about privacy violation is the cookie. The cookie feature was created by Netscape as part of its browser. Cookies are ASCII files (plain text) that can be created and accessed by a Web site visited by the browser. The file is resident in the browser directory, so if the Web site visitor decides to use another browser, the cookie won't be readable by the originating Web site. The visitor can also delete cookies or disable the browser feature that creates them. The benefit of the feature is that the cookie file lets the site being visited know something about visitors and their interests by accessing it, and it permits the site to provide custom-designed information based on the cookie file. Having a cookie can save a lot of time and keystrokes, because the site will "recognize" the visitor as a repeat visitor and "remember" what he or she did on previous visits. The downside is that the visitor may not wish to share this information and may not even know that cookie files are being created.

> Privacy, security, intellectual property protection, and regulation of Internet fundraising pose challenges to the online fundraiser. You need to keep current with the latest developments relating to all of these issues.

Many see the Internet culture as a threat to privacy concerns. Obviously, nonprofits and for-profit organizations alike accrue substantial benefit in collecting and sharing data about their Web site visitors. But is the cost to society of unfettered data collection and dissemination too high? Should the responsibility for regulating privacy on the Internet fall chiefly to state governments or the federal government? Is self-regulation by the industry a reasonable alternative to legislation? Should Web sites require that visitors prospectively "opt-in" by expressly pre-authorizing the site to collect data, or merely to "opt-out" to prohibit data from being collected (with the "default" decision being that permission is assumed to be granted)?

Regulators at the state and federal levels are wrestling with how to strike a balance between the legitimate needs of organizations to collect data and forestalling unwarranted intrusion into our personal lives. Nonprofit organizations have a stake in the outcome of this debate. On one hand, our sector benefits from collecting and sharing data. On the other hand, we are often the only organized advocate for vulnerable and exploited populations.

It is not yet clear the direction the online privacy debate is headed. But the trend is for those who collect information from Web site visitors, including nonprofit organizations, to develop and publish a policy stating how this information is used. If you are using your Web site to collect information of any kind from your site's visitors, a written, formal privacy policy is becoming a necessity, if only to protect your organization from potential legal liability.

A Web site privacy policy generally includes—

1. *What information provided by Web site visitors will be shared with others, and under what circumstances.* For example, many organizations sell or rent their mailing lists and databases.

2. *What information will not be shared with others.* For example, a telephone number may be required for credit card verification. While many business organizations will request the telephone number for that purpose (or to communicate with the customer in the event there is a problem with the transaction), they will not release the customer's telephone number to outsiders.

3. *What customers can do to keep their names, addresses, and other data confidential.* This may entail simply checking a box on an electronic form.

4. *What information is being collected without the direct knowledge of the Web site visitor.* The use of cookies has become a standard practice, and a privacy policy should explain how cookies will be used.

Examples of privacy policies

Almost all of the reputable nonprofit organizations on the Web have a privacy policy. For example, you can examine the policy of the Metropolitan Museum of New York (*http://www.metmuseum.org*). From the home page, click on "Met Store." From the menu on the left of the screen, near the bottom, click on "customer service." Then click on "online privacy" from the menu in the middle of the screen. Then click on "privacy policy" on the middle of the screen. This policy is comprehensive and will provide you with plenty of issues to think about when designing your online privacy policy.

For an example of a privacy policy for a membership organization's Web site, and one that is more accessible from the home page, surf to the site of the National Association of Attorneys General (NAAG): *http://www.naag.org*. Click on "privacy policy" from the menu at the bottom of the page. This organization has formulated a draft set of principles on Internet privacy, and thus would be expected to have a privacy policy that is based on those principles. As you might imagine, the draft NAAG principles are not supported by prominent members of the Online Privacy Alliance, a coalition that includes

Microsoft, IBM, AOL Time Warner, and scores of other associations and individual companies (see the Alliance's own privacy policy at: *http://www.privacyalliance.org/resources/ppguidelines.shtml*)

Protection of Customer Data

Virtually every survey has demonstrated the pervasive fear consumers have with respect to providing their credit card numbers over the Internet. The concern that unscrupulous merchants (or those who pretend to be merchants) will use the credit card information is mostly unfounded; even if this happened (and it does occasionally), there are limits on the amount of loss the consumer sustains (typically $50), and there is typically no exposure to loss if the problem is reported promptly. The principal concern tends to be that hackers will somehow tap into the transaction and steal the credit card data. It is probably a more likely occurrence that credit card data is stolen simply as a result of people, both merchants and consumers, being careless with the paper records of these transactions. Nonetheless, a lot of effort has gone into making financial transactions over the Internet safe by encrypting (that is, disguising) the data so that only the intended sender and receiver can read it.

While there are several protocols for encryption, the industry standard for e-commerce has become Secure Sockets Layer, or SSL. It uses what's known as a public and private key system and the use of a digital certificate.

Without having both the public and private keys, a message that is encrypted looks like gobbledygook. Each person has his or her own private key, which is kept very secret, and a public key, which is shared with everyone. The messages cannot be read without having both. Thus, if you send an encrypted message to someone and use their public key, you cannot even read the encrypted message yourself because you don't have access to their private key.

Popular encryption programs

Two popular encryption programs are available. PGP, or Pretty Good Privacy, can be found at *http://www.pgp.com.* It can be downloaded for commercial use for a modest fee. A similar program that does not use sophisticated algorithms subject to Department of Commerce export restrictions has also been developed. GnuPG is available for free at the following site: *http://www.gnupg.org.*

There is an excellent Web site that explains encryption in more detail at:

http://webmonkey.wired.com/webmonkey/programming/php/tutorials/tutorial1.html

Certification/Authentication

If you are serious about accepting credit cards on your Web site, you should obtain an SSL certificate from a certifying authority to assure donors that you are who you say you are and your server is secure. A donor can see a lock icon on the browser that indicates that the page is encrypted. Most people will refuse to send their credit card information over the Internet unless you have a valid certificate. Server certificates are available commercially from many different companies, and the cost varies.

The most widely used authority in the United States is VeriSign *(http://www.verisign.com/)*. Competing companies include Thawte Consulting *(http://www.thawte.com)*, and Entrust *(http://www.entrust.com)*. One recurring problem is that the certificates may not work on all browsers, so make sure to inquire about this.

You can have all of the sophisticated encryption systems in place, but it won't do any good if you keep the printouts of credit card numbers on your desk, or put them in an accessible file on your computer that is not password-protected. Take reasonable precautions to keep your customer data protected.

Firewalls

Firewall is a term that describes Internet security software that controls access between two or more computer networks (e.g., your organization's computer network and the Internet), allowing approved traffic in and out through a secure gateway. Firewall software can be downloaded free from the Internet or can be obtained for thousands of dollars. See *http://www.interhack.net/pubs/fwfaq/* for a complete guide to firewalls.

Copyright Law

While a detailed discussion of copyright law is beyond the scope of this book, nonprofit managers who use the Internet need to be concerned about this for plenty of reasons. First, nonprofit organizations post lots of materials on their Web pages that they don't necessarily want to see reproduced and disseminated without their permission. Second, nonprofit managers use a lot of material they find on the World Wide Web, which may or may not be copyrighted. It is important to have an understanding of how these materials may be legally used. Third, nonprofit managers send e-mail and post messages to online message boards, mailing lists, and chat rooms. You may word something differently if you know that a publisher can include, as a direct quote in a book with a 100,000 first printing, something that you innocently posted on your donor recognition page.

Several Web sites keep up with Internet controversies involving what has been labeled "intellectual property"—patents, trademarks, and copyrights. Among the better sites are: U.S. Copyright Office *(http://www.copyright.gov/)* and Brad Templeton's "Ten Big Myths About Copyright Explained *(http://www.templetons.com/brad/copymyths.html)*.

Regulation of Online Fundraising

The use of the Internet for fundraising has raised legal questions that previously were not relevant. For example, is a charity in Pennsylvania that is not registered in Utah violating the Utah solicitation law if it puts a general solicitation on its Web site and receives contributions from someone in Utah? This area of law is not clear, and it will likely take several years, if not decades, for a body of case law and statutory law to provide guidance to charities wrestling with these questions.

Beginning in the late 1990s, the National Association of Attorneys General (NAAG) and the National Association of State Charity Officials (NASCO) began meeting to reach a consensus national policy on how states should appropriately regulate charitable solicitation conducted over the Internet. The public dialogue on this issue began in Charleston, S.C. at the October 1999 NAAG/NASCO annual conference. A final version was approved in 2001. For details, point your Web browser to:
http://www.afpnet.org/ka/ka-3.cfm?content_item_id=2324&folder_id=893)

Charities that shied away from putting solicitation information on their Web sites for fear of attracting out-of-state enforcement proceedings can breathe a bit easier and feel comfortable reposting this information. Charities that took the time and effort (and considerable expense) to register in all of the 40 states requiring registration may reconsider whether the extent to which they solicit falls within the thresholds of these principles. And charities that target their Internet solicitations to out-of-state residents, either via their Web pages or e-mail, should be put on notice that these direct and indirect solicitations will, rightfully so, be treated the same as charitable solicitations conducted by conventional media.

Charities should note that these principles are advisory only, and are not binding on any individual state regulator.

Conclusion

Problems with respect to privacy, security, use of intellectual property, and state regulation still remain when using the Internet for fundraising. But there are many committed folks working hard to solve these problems. We feel that all things considered, using the Internet for fundraising has much greater benefits than risks, provided you use common sense and take adequate precautions.

Resources

Brad Templeton's *10 Big Myths About Copyright Explained*
http://www.templetons.com/brad/copymyths.html

Last updated in October 2004, this document explains what you can and cannot do with respect to using the works of others. For a primer on copyright, see his related page at: *http://www.templetons.com/brad/copyright.html*

Cornell Law School's Legal Information Institute
http://www.law.cornell.edu/topics/copyright.html

This page includes legal citations for copyright laws, court decisions, and international conventions, many in full text, and links to groups, organizations, publications, and government agencies with an interest in copyright developments. This is a good example of a Web site that is designed poorly yet has valuable content.

David Whalen The Unofficial Cookie FAQ
http://www.cookiecentral.com/faq/

This document could have been called "Everything You Wanted To Know About Cookies But Were Afraid To Ask." It is a soup-to-nuts encyclopedia covering what they are, how they work, why they exist, and how to create them for your Web site. Must reading for anyone interested in the privacy issue (and, if you ever ask us if we are interested, we'll tell you that it's none of your business!). The site was last updated in 2002, but the information still looks quite useful.

The Electronic Privacy Information Center
http://www.epic.org

This site has plenty of valuable resources, as well as links to other useful materials.

Europe's Organisation for Economic Cooperation and Development (OECD) Privacy Policy Statement Generator
http://www.oecd.org/document/39/0,2340,en_2649_34255_28863271_1_1_1_1,00.html

This site provides a useful tool for developing privacy policies, utilizing a questionnaire to help you assess how you use personal data.

GNU Privacy Guard
http://www.gnupg.org

This is the site where you can download free privacy software and the manual that goes with it.

The Interhack Web—Internet Firewalls
http://www.interhack.net/pubs/fwfaq

This is a comprehensive FAQ file on Internet firewalls prepared by Matt Curtin and Marcus Ranum, computer science researchers, and last updated in 2004.

Network Associates' Pretty Good Privacy (PGP)
http://www.pgp.com

This commercial site is the vendor of the leading encryption and firewall software.

State Regulation of Internet Solicitation
http://www.muridae.com/nporegulation/documents/internet_solicitation_law.html

This page accesses Paul E. Monaghan, Jr.'s 1996 paper from Yale Law School titled *Charitable Solicitation Over the Internet and State-Law Restrictions*, written under the direction of Professor John Simon. Clear, concise, and provocative, but, alas, more than a decade out of date.

TRUSTe
http://www.truste.org

TRUSTe is an organization that was established in 1996 to set up privacy standards and provide sanctions against its participants that violate the standards. Web sites that meet TRUSTe's strict privacy standards in the areas of notice, choice, access, and security and submit to TRUSTe's oversight program can display the organization's logo. It has become the Web privacy equivalent of the "Good Housekeeping Seal of Approval." The fee is based on annual revenue, and ranges from $599 for organizations with annual revenue of up to $1 million to $12,999 for organizations with over $2 billion in annual revenue.

Uniform Registration Statement Page
http://www.multistatefiling.org/

This page provides access to a printable version (in PDF format) of the latest version (3.01 as of February 2006) Uniform Registration Statement (URS), which is accepted by 35 states and the District of Columbia. Eight of these states and D.C. require a supplemental form, which is also available at this site). This form is useful to charities that solicit charitable contributions in multiple states. The page also has FAQ files and an HTML file of the URS, which is useful for reading on a computer screen. The FAQ details the registration requirements in all states and DC.

U.S. Copyright Office
http://www.lcweb.loc.gov/copyright

This site has all of the documents and forms you need to register your copyrights, and includes links to applicable laws, federal regulations, and treaties. Be sure to read the FAQ document at: *http://www.loc.gov/copyright/faq.html*

U.S. Patent and Trademark Office
http://www.uspto.gov/main/trademarks.htm

This is the official information page for the federal government office that administers trademark law. You can register for a trademark online at this site, check the status of a pending or existing trademark, or find basic information about the process and the law.

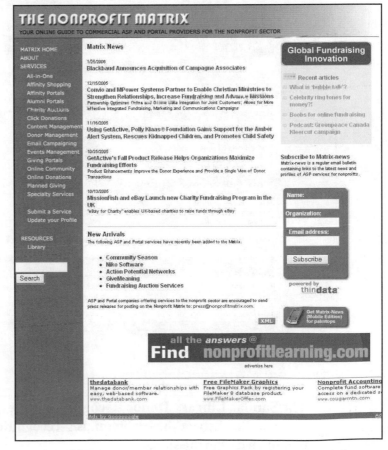

The Nonprofit Matrix home page at: http://www.nonprofitmatrix.com. Reprinted with permission.

Sanilac
District Library

Home | Services | Library Info | Links | New Material | Hours | Location | Site Index

Recognition of Gifts
"Growing To Meet Your Needs"

All Donors to our "Growing To Meet Your Needs" fund will be publicly acknowledged (unless anonymity is requested) and permanently recognized in the library and on our Website. Check out our "Ways to Give" Page for more information.

"The Giving Tree"	
Contribution	**Recognition**
$20,000-$24,999.....Name Engraved on Acorn	
$15,000-$19,999.....Name Engraved on Large Foundation Stone	
$10,000-$14,999........Name Engraved on Medium Foundation Stone	
$5,000-$9,999.........Name Engraved on Small Foundation Stone	
$1,000-$4,999........Name Engraved on Gold Leaf	
$500-$999..............Name Engraved on Silver Leaf	
$100-$499..............Name Engraved on Bronze Leaf	
$1-$99...................Name Inscribed in Book of Remembrance	

A Special Thank You to Those Who Made Contributions and Wish to Remain Anonymous.

Foundation Stone Donations	
Joe Casanovas	Jay & Kae Hartford
Ford & Lulu Derby	William & Pamela Weiner

Foundation Stone Donations Given In Loving Memory Of
Marian McNaughton Hoffman "Who Loved To Read"

Gold Level Contributions	
Susan & Rick Akkerman	Barbara Logan
Harold & Marguery Allen	Jane Logan
Curt & Linda Backus	Virginia Logan
Sophia Backus	Phil & Alice Marsom
Cabinets & Creations	MI Aviation Education Foundation
Bill & Paula Cayce	Cynthia & Joe Mooney
William & Gail Coyne	Nancy Walters Aviation Section
Bob & Bev Dear	Port Sanilac DDA
Ray & Shirley Denison	Pomeroy Funeral Home
Exchange State Bank	Project Blessing
Extang Corporation	William Ruhstorfer
Gary Fetting	Diane & Steve Schneider
Chester & CeAnn Kolascz	Robert & Charlyne Stasiuk
Bob & Annette Konupek	

Gold Level Contributions Given In Loving Memory of	
Fran Bulone	Lenora Payne
Mildred Clark	Rick J. Ouellette
Leota Cross	Virginia Raymond Tubbs
Lulu Derby	Ludwik N. & Helena L. Witkowski

The Sanilac Library Donor Recognition Page (excerpt) at http://www.sanilacdistrictlibrary.lib.mi.us/g-recognition.html. Reprinted with permission.

Appendix A: Sections of a Grant Application

1. Cover Letter

Many grant applications specifically request a cover letter and define what information should be included. If this is not expressly prohibited by the grant application format, write a short cover letter on the organization's stationery that:

- Is addressed to the appropriate individual at the grantor agency, making sure the name, title, agency name, and address are absolutely correct.

- Contains a one-sentence description of the proposal.

- Provides the number of participants, jobs obtained, or other units to be funded by the grant.

- Lists the total amount of funds requested.

- Provides the name, address, and telephone number of the individual at the requesting organization the grantor can contact to request additional information.

2. Executive Summary

Include in this section a succinct summary of the entire proposal.

3. Introduction

Provide important information that may not otherwise appear anywhere else in the grant application. Items you might include are—

- Your organization's mission
- How long you have been providing the type of service included in this program
- Brief history of your organization
- Major indicators that you are capable of operating programs efficiently and effectively
- If there are eligibility requirements in the proposal, a statement that you are eligible to receive the funds
- IRS Section 501(c) tax-exempt status determination letter
- Outline of letters of support from past clients, representatives of cooperating agencies, and legislative officials (The letters themselves should be included as appendices to the application.)

- Statement of how you will obtain funding for the program at the end of the grant period.

4. Need

For a grant to be funded, the organization must demonstrate the need of individuals in the community for the service to be provided. What is the extent of the need and how is the need documented? The need described should be the need of the individuals in the community for the services, not the need of the organization. Rather than stating, "We need a counselor because our organization doesn't have one," or "The funds for the one we had were cut back by the government," estimate the number of individuals who need counseling services. The need should be the need in your coverage area. While national or statewide figures might be given, if you serve a particular county, the estimate of need for that county should be provided.

The need should be the need for the particular service you are providing. If you provide services for victims of domestic violence, for example, the estimated number of victims of domestic violence should be provided, rather than unemployment figures or other available statistics. The need should be quantified. How many individuals do you believe are eligible for the particular service you provide in your coverage area?

Common sources of data are—

a. **Census Data**—Make certain you are using data from the most recent census. In most cases, earlier data are outdated.

b. **County Planning Departments**—Call the office of your county government to find the telephone number for your county's planning department.

c. **State Agencies**—The Departments of Education, Health, Labor, and Human Services, or their equivalents, are all excellent sources of data.

d. **Local Governments**—Local police departments are excellent sources of crime data, and local school districts can provide educational information.

e. **Self-generated data**—In many cases, you can provide the data from sources within your organization. Sources might include—

- Waiting lists
- Letters from potential clients requesting a service
- Letters complaining that a particular service is not in existence

- Testimony at public hearings
- Information obtained from questionnaires administered to present clients asking them to list other services they might like
- Community surveys.

5. Objectives

Objectives are the proposed results of the project. Objectives should have the following characteristics:

- They are measurable. How many individuals do you estimate will participate in your program?

- They are time-based. How many individuals do you estimate will participate in your program in the next three months? In the next year?

- They are realistic.

The information needed to measure objectives can be obtained as part of the program funded by the grant. Do not list objectives in your proposal that are impossible to measure.

6. Project Description

Here is where you will outline your program. An easy way to remember what to include are the 6 W's of program writing:

a. Who? Who are the clients? How are they selected? What are the restrictions (e.g., age, income, geographic)? Who are the staff members?

If you are asking the funding source to pay for new staff members, include a job description and a qualifications statement that lists the education, experience, and other job requirements. If you are applying for funds for existing staff, include a résumé and a biographical statement for each staff member.

b. What? What services will be provided? What will the benefits of this program be? What are the expected outcomes? For educational programs, include a course outline. You may include relevant sections of an operations manual. For other programs, a narrative outlining the services would be appropriate. Still others might provide a "day in the life of a client." What outreach efforts will be made?

c. Where? Where will the services be provided? Give the addresses of all main and field offices. If you will be obtaining new space with the program funds, what type of space are you seeking?

d. When? What are the hours that services will be provided? On which days during the year will services be provided? It is also useful to provide a time-table for project implementation.

e. With whom? What other agencies are participating with you in the provision of services? For example, include agencies referring clients to you. Outline the agencies to which you refer clients. It is important to obtain letters from the other agencies confirming any relationships you describe.

f. Why? Why are you providing these services rather than alternatives? Are you utilizing any unique approaches to the provision of services?

7. Budget

If it is not clear from the grant application forms, ask the funding source how much financial detail is required. Many businesses, for example, may only require the total amount you are going to spend. On the other hand, most government agencies require a line-item budget that includes a detailed estimate of all funds to be spent. Such a budget might be set up to include the following:

a. Personnel costs (salaries, fringe benefits, consultant and contract services)

b. Non-personnel costs (travel, office space, equipment, consumable supplies, and other costs such as telephone, postage, and indirect costs)

Some grantors may require your organization to contribute a matching share. If you are permitted to include in-kind or non-cash expenditures, use the same budget categories as above. In the personnel category, for example, you would list the worth of the time volunteers are contributing to your program. In the non-personnel category, you would include the market value of the equipment donated to your program.

8. Evaluation

Inform the funding source that you will be conducting an evaluation of the services you are providing.

a. Detail who will participate in the evaluation process. Outline the participation of board members, staff members, clients, experts in the substantive field, and representatives of the community in the evaluation process. Some grantors require an independent evaluator.

b. Explain what will be evaluated. List some of the issues the evaluation team will consider. For example, the evaluators will review whether the need was reduced as a result of providing the services. Were the objectives met? Were the services provided as outlined in the Project Description section? Will the budget be audited by an outside firm and, if not, who will review the receipts and expenditures?

c. Specify what type of evaluation will be provided. Provide in as much detail as you can how the program will be evaluated. If formal classes are provided, include the pre- and post-test you will use to evaluate them.

If a client questionnaire will be used, attach a copy to the application. Describe how the program data will be reviewed in the evaluation process. Include a description of the audit or the process you will use to review the budget items.

9. Conclusion

In no more than two or three paragraphs, summarize the proposal's main points and the reasons the community will be improved as a result of successful completion of the project.

When you have finished writing your grant application, ask yourself the following questions before you send it to the funding source:

- Is the application free of the jargon of your field?
- Are all abbreviations spelled out the first time you use them?
- Have you followed all of the instructions in the Request for Proposal (RFP)?
- Are all words spelled correctly? Remember that your computer's spell-checker only tells you that the words you use are spelled correctly and in English, not that they are the correct words for the context.
- Is your application interesting to read?
- If you were the grantor agency, would you fund it?

Finally, get the application in the hands of the grantor well before the deadline. The fundraising field is replete with horror stories about multi-million dollar proposals that were not even considered because someone put the application in the mail and it didn't arrive until well after the deadline. Make sure there is enough postage if the application is mailed. It is highly recommended that applications be either hand-delivered or sent by a trackable, overnight courier, such as Federal Express or Airborne Express. Make several office copies before submitting the original, and be sure that you provide the number of copies requested by the grantor.

If permitted (some grantors even require this), submit the proposal electronically.

This Appendix is adapted from *The Nonprofit Handbook* (4th Edition) and was written by Michael A. Sand, Esq., a private nonprofit consultant based in Harrisburg, PA.

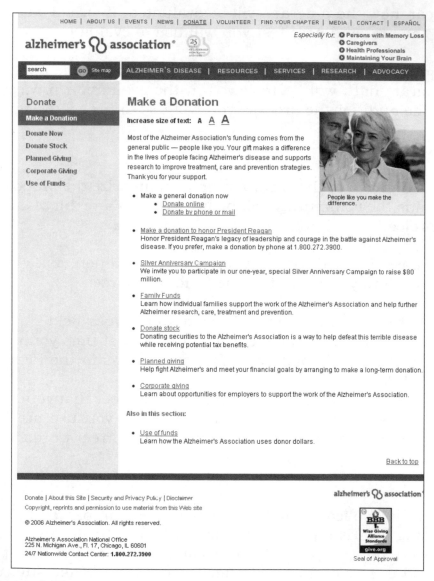

The Alzheimer's Association Online Donation page at http://www.alz.org/Donate/overview.asp. Reprinted with permission.

Appendix B: Open Source Software

Firefox. Joomla. Linux. MySQL. You've probably heard these names of software products in the news recently, and maybe even tried them out. They are all high quality, top of the line, and useful to most nonprofit organizations for a variety of applications. And they have something in common that makes them even more of a value to cost-conscious charities. They are all FREE for downloading and installation on as many computers as you have, and can be modified and distributed by you or others without having to obtain permission from the original developers.

These are all examples of what is known as "open source" software.

Open source software is quickly becoming the choice of thousands of charities for applications including operating systems (Linux), browsers (Firefox), databases (MySQL), and Web site design (Joomla). And because their developers have chosen to make the source code publicly available, these programs can be modified to meet customized needs and encourage the development of add-ons and related modifications that are designed with your organization's needs in mind.

What is Open Source Software

The term refers to software whose source code is public, so it can be modified without obtaining permission. Often, the software is licensed to users using a standardized form (see *http://www.opensource.org/licenses/gpl-license.php* for the text of the GNU's General Public License—GNU/GPL— the industry standard for licensing open source software) that sets the rules for development and use of open source software. Software licensed by the GNU/GPL is free to use or modify.

This contrasts to "freeware," which is also free, but typically requires a license to use and distribute and prohibits the user from modifying the source code, which is typically kept proprietary. It is also different from "shareware," software sold on a "try before you buy" model. Shareware or free trial software can be downloaded for free and tried out for a limited period of time before you are requested to make a payment to the developer in order to continue using it.

Open source software is a model that encourages volunteers to collaborate not for the purpose of making money, but to improve software for the common good. Unlike almost all efforts of commercial software developers, there is a clear altruism in the open source philosophy, not just a cynical marketing ploy as some have charged about the efforts of proprietary software developers.

As we write this, hundreds of open source projects are underway involving thousands of volunteers, all committed to meeting your software needs and those of others without any expectation of benefit to themselves other than personal satisfaction and the thrill of collaborating with others to make a good product even better.

Advantages of Open Source Software

There are a lot of advantages of choosing open source software over competing proprietary software packages. Among them are—

1. The software is distributed freely with no charge to either purchase it outright or license its use.
2. You can put the software on as many computers as you like.
3. Software developers, for a fee or for free, are continually modifying the software to increase its applicability to customized applications, eliminate bugs, and improve its performance and versatility.
4. You don't have to pay for periodic updates.
5. There are no marketing gimmicks that one typically finds embedded in the source code of proprietary software.
6. If a commercial vendor goes out of business, there are no future upgrades and no one to provide support or training. Open source software can be immortal and organic, capable of being improved and supported by a community long after the original developer has moved on to other projects (if there is an active community of users and developers).

Disadvantages of Open Source Software

However, there are disadvantages as well. Among these are—

1. There may not be a stable source of support for a software program, such as that usually provided by a commercial vendor; support generally comes from volunteer posters on bulletin boards devoted to an open source product. (Actually, many see this as an advantage rather than a disadvantage.)
2. The software may not run on all operating systems.
3. There are fewer published books about how to use open source software compared to proprietary software packages, at least for now, and the software's documentation may be incomplete.
4. There may not be the same level of quality control for add-ons to open source software as there is for proprietary competitors, since anyone can change the source code and market a customized application, regardless of their technical sophistication and whether anyone else has sufficiently debugged that application.
5. The products are constantly being developed by volunteers, and new versions may be released frequently or willy-nilly. These frequent releases may be

viewed as either a positive or a negative. In contrast, with proprietary software, there is an incentive to release new versions only periodically when market conditions are ripe. If an open source application is headed by one "guru" who suddenly loses interest and no one decides to pick up the project, that application could die out.

So What Does All of This Have to Do With Penguins?

A penguin is the logo for Linux, the most popular open source operating system. Several times each year, Penguin Day is held in a different city (the first two took place in March 2004 in Philadelphia and May 7, 2005 in New York City), bringing together open source software developers and technology staff of nonprofit organizations. The mission of the coalition that organizes these conferences, Penguinday.org, is to foster networking among nonprofit technology users and provide a forum by which software developers with a social conscience can help nonprofits. Penguinday.org is supported by a grant from the IBM Corporation and other corporate sponsors. Penguin Day is the brainchild of three organizations: Aspiration *(http://www.aspirationtech.org)*, the Nonprofit Open Source initiative (NOSI) *(http://www.nosi.net)*, and the LINC Project of the Welfare Law Center *(http://www.lincproject.org)*.

Penguin days begin and expand the process by which charities communicate their software needs to those with the talent to fulfill those needs. There is a modest registration fee to participate, which can be waived for those who cannot afford it. See the Penguinday.org Web site for more details and upcoming schedules of future Penguin days.

Why the Open Source Movement is Important for Charities

America's charities, as they did in the early 1980s, are again bracing for a two-edged sword of Damocles above their heads—a sharp decrease in government spending for social programs and a corresponding steep increase in the demand for the services they provide. For a sector that has relatively minuscule resources to begin with, the challenge continues to make sure that every dollar is channeled efficiently and effectively.

In our previous writings, we have trumpeted the value of various Web sites that help charities stretch their dollars with respect to obtaining free and discounted hardware and software. Many of these sites are still going strong. For example, you can still use your 501(c)(3) status to obtain heavily discounted popular commercial software such as Microsoft Office and Macromedia Dreamweaver at TechSoup's DiscounTech Stock *(http://www.techsoup.com/stock)*, and find resources to receive surplus computers at *http://opencollector.org/freecomputers.html* and *http://www.recycles.org/*. These are still excellent ways to bridge the digital divide. But the open source movement has perhaps more potential to create a level technology playing field in the nonprofit sector and help us reach our full potential by harnessing the benefits of computer technology. And it's nice to know that the philosophy driving this movement is consonant with the sector's core values of furthering the common good rather than individual economic gain.

This Appendix is based on an article by Gary Grobman that first appeared in *Contributions Magazine* in May 2005.

The Hoover's home page at http://www.hoovers.com/ free. Reprinted with permission. See page 56 for a review of this site.

Appendix C: Example of an Electronic Newsletter
Excerpt from Philanthropy News Digest Electronic Newsletter (Reprinted With Permission)

=======================================
PHILANTHROPY NEWS DIGEST
   a service of the Foundation Center
=======================================

February 21, 2006   Volume 12, Issue 8

To subscribe or unsubscribe, or to change your e-mail address, visit: http://fdncenter.org/newsletters/

This week's PND Poll wants to know: Is your organization a good collaborator?

To cast your vote, visit: http://fdncenter.org/pnd/

::::::::::::::: OPINION & COMMENTARY :::::::::::::::

PND invites and publishes opinion and commentary by foundation and nonprofit leaders on topics important to the philanthropic sector. For more information, visit: http://fdncenter.org/pnd/opinion/

***************** ADVERTISEMENT **********************
ONLINE FUNDRAISING MADE EASY
Firstgiving's fundraising web pages make it easy for your supporters to raise funds for you. Let them set up their own Firstgiving page and reach their own network of donors. Incredibly simple and effective, Firstgiving pages are perfect for fundraising events or ongoing appeals. See how Firstgiving pages are already being used: http://fconline.fdncenter.org/pnd/10001028/firstgiving

Contact Firstgiving at 781-863-6166, X105, or e-mail inquiries@firstgiving.com.
::::::::::::::: IN THEIR OWN WORDS :::::::::::::::
"Foundations are clearly in an era of public scrutiny because we are growing in size and service, and in
 public awareness."
-- Steve Gunderson, president of the D.C.-based Council on Foundations (New York Times 2/11/06)

:::::::::::::::: IN THE NEWS :::::::::::::::::
The Web version of PND offers abstracts of philanthropy news items each day. The following are the top stories from the past week and their date of posting.
(1) California AG Questions Getty Severance Packages   (2/15/06)
(2) Voluntary Gifts to Colleges, Universities Up 4.9 Percent in 2005 (2/21/06)
(3) Federal Dollars to Faith-Based Groups Decline, Study Finds (2/17/06)
(4) Kellogg Foundation Selects Twelve Universities for
      Initiative to Eliminate Health Disparities (2/21/06)
(5) Mott Foundation to Support Automotive Industry (2/17/06)
(6) St. Paul Foundation Launches Initiative to Address Racism (2/20/06)
(7) Jim Joseph Foundation Receives $500 Million Bequest (2/16/06)
(8) Bank of America to Award $200 Million in 2006 (2/21/06)
(9) Stanford to Receive $30 Million for Environmental Institute (2/18/06)
(10) People in the News: Appointments and Promotions (2/19/06)

:::::::::::::::: MORE NEWS :::::::::::::::::

(11) Silicon Valley Nonprofit Sector Grew Between 1994 and 2003 (2/15/06)
(12) Venture Capitalist Invests in Education Reform (2/17/06)
(13) Younger Celebrities Reach Out to Smaller, Little-Known Charities (2/16/06)
(14) Nonprofits Leave Southeastern Michigan United Way Pension Plan (2/15/06)
(15) Fifteen Pennsylvania Nonprofits Join Forces to Build Community Center (2/17/06)
(16) Minnesota Power Establishes Charitable Foundation (2/18/06)
(17) University of the Ozarks to Receive $20 Million for Teacher Education Program (2/20/06)
(18) University of Wisconsin-Milwaukee to Receive $10 Million for Business School (2/19/06)

(19) UM Museum of Art Annouces $6.5 Million in Gifts for Expansion Project (2/15/06)
(20) Frey Foundation Commits $5 Million to Fight Homelessness (2/16/06)
(21) Smithfield-Luter Foundation Awards $5 Million to University of Virginia Health System (2/18/06)
(22) University of North Carolina, Duke to Receive $1.65 Million for Teacher Education Program (2/20/06)
(23) Wachovia Foundation Awards $1 Million to Assist Urban, College-Bound Students in Texas Schools (2/20/06)
(24) Bank of America to Award $750,000 to Expand New York City Child-Vaccination Program (2/19/06)
----

(1) California AG Questions Getty Severance Packages (2/15/06)
 In the wake of the resignation of its president and CEO. Barry Munitz, the J. Paul Getty Trust (http://getty.edu/) remains under investigation by the California attorney general's office, which has questions about the trust's finances, including whether excessive severance packages were paid to two senior executives, the New York Times reports.

 According to two former Getty officials, one of the executives, Deborah Gribbon -- who resigned in the fall of 2004 as director of the Getty Museum after a series of disagreements with Munitz -- was given a $3 million severance package, almost nine times her base salary of $350,000. The other executive, Jill Murphy, who served as Munitz's chief of staff, was paid $250,000 in severance after she agreed to leave the trust late last year. According to experts, the payments may violate federal tax laws governing spending by tax-exempt institutions, which specify that such institutions must use their resources to benefit the public good. Investigators were also looking into several instances in which Munitz had authorized grants or uses of the trust's money without obtaining proper approval. In some cases, the money was spent on pet projects of his that had very little to do with the Getty's mission.

 "Foundations are clearly in an era of public scrutiny because we are growing in size and service, and in public awareness," said Steve Gunderson, president of the Washington, D.C.-based Council on Foundations, which placed the Getty, the nation's third-largest private foundation, on probation in December as questions about its spending became public. Munitz's resignation, added Gunderson, "sends a signal to this sector to take steps to police itself."

 Kennedy, Randy. Vogel, Carol. "Executives Severance Is a Focus at Getty." New York Times 2/11/06.
  http://fconline.fdncenter.org/pnd/10001031/story
 ------------------------<<>>------------------------
(2) Voluntary Gifts to Colleges, Universities Up 4.9 Percent in 2005 (2/21/06)

 Contributions to colleges and universities in the United States grew by 4.9 percent in 2005, reaching $25.6 billion, a survey from the Council for Aid to Education (http://www.cae.org/) finds.

 According to the annual Voluntary Support of Education, the increase was driven largely by gifts from alumni, as well as a strong boost from foundations and other support- ing organizations. Nearly half the funds raised by colleges and universities in 2005 came directly from individuals. Alumni giving, the traditional base of higher education support, grew by 6 percent in 2005, while giving by individuals other than alumni, which was up by 21.5 percent in 2004, declined by 3.8 percent in 2005.

 The survey also found that Stanford University raised more from private donors ($603.6 million) than any other university, followed by the University of Wisconsin ($595.2 mil lion), which received a one-time gift of $296 million as the result of the conversion of Blue Cross & Blue Shield United of Wisconsin from nonprofit to for-profit status, and Harvard ($589.9 million).

 "The results indicate that giving to higher education con tinues to recover from the weak performances of 2002 and 2003," said Ann E. Kaplan, director of the survey. "The increase in giving to just the top ten universities accounts for half of the total growth in higher education giving in 2005."

 "Contributions to Colleges and Universities Up by 4.9 percent to $25.6 Billion." Council forAid to Education Survey 2/16/06.
  http://fconline.fdncenter.org/pnd/10001033/story
 ------------------------<<>>------------------------
(3) Federal Dollars to Faith-Based Groups Decline, Study Finds (2/17/06)
 A new study finds that, despite the Bush administration's vocal support for faith-based charities, the dollar total of direct federal grants to faith-based organizations declined from 2002 to 2004, the Washington Post reports. Conducted by the Roundtable on Religion and Social Welfare Policy (http://www.religionandsocialpolicy.org/about/) in Albany, New York, the study examined 28,000 grants made
 by nine federal agencies over three years and found that faith-based charities received an unchanging share -- about 18 percent -- of the funds awarded each year. But because the total amount available shrank by more than $230 million over that period, the amount going to religious groups also declined, from $670 million in fiscal 2002 to $626 million in fiscal 2004. At the same time, the study found, the president's faith-based initiative succeeded in encouraging more religious groups to apply for funding, boosting the number that received grants by almost 15 percent.

 The study, which was authored by Lisa M. Montiel and David J. Wright, focused only on direct federal grants, not those distributed through block grants to states and muni cipalities, and only included programs that existed over the duration of the three-year period.

 White House officials disputed the study's findings, say ing their own figures, which they will release next month, show an increase in funding. H. James Towey, director of the White House Office of Faith-Based and Community Initiatives, noted that the study also ignored programs like Head Start, which Towey said was the second-largest source of federal funds for faith-based organizations, after the

Department of Housing and Urban Development's Section 202 housing program for the elderly poor.

Candy S. Hill, senior vice president for social services at Catholic Charities USA in Alexandria, Virginia, said the study's findings fit with her experience. "It doesn't surprise me, because overall the funding for most social service programs is shrinking," she said. "We're grateful there's a recognition by the administration of the wonderful work that faith-based groups do, but we continue to be concerned about the levels of funding."

Cooperman, Alan. "Grants to Religious Groups Fall, Study Says." Washington Post 2/15/06.
  http://fconline.fdncenter.org/pnd/10001034/story
  -------------------------<<>>------------------------
(4) Kellogg Foundation Selects Twelve Universities for Initiative to Eliminate Health Disparities (2/21/06)
The W.K. Kellogg Foundation (http://www.wkkf.org) in Battle Creek, Michigan, has chosen twelve schools and graduate programs of public health to participate in its Engaged Institutions initiative to focus on eliminating racial and ethnic health disparities.
Arising from a seminar sponsored by the foundation, the initiative will bring together the institutions and their communities as partners to build upon their strengths and capacities to address the health disparities that persist between whites and people of color. For example, not only are most racial and ethnic groups less healthy than their white counterparts, but they also tend to have shorter life expectancies, higher rates of infant mortality and chronic diseases, worse outcomes once diagnosed with illnesses, and less access to health care.

Community-Campus Partnerships for Health, at the University of Washington in Seattle, will work collaboratively with teams from each school -- made up of academic administrators, faculty, staff, students, and community partners -- as they develop and implement their strategic plans. It will also provide additional support through the CCPH Consultancy Network, its training and technical assistance arm. In addition, the initiative will sponsor teleconferences, identify promising practices, and produce resource materials.

The following schools and their graduate public health programs will take part in the initiative: the University of Arizona, the University of Arkansas for Medical Sciences, San Jose State University (California), the University of South Florida, the University of Hawaii, Morgan State University (Maryland), Boston University, the University of Nebraska, the University of North Carolina, the University of South Carolina, Virginia Commonwealth University, and an Oregon consortium comprised of Portland State University, Oregon Health and Science University, and Oregon State University.

"12 Schools and Graduate Programs of Public Health Selected for Engaged Institutions Initiative Focused on Eliminating Health Disparities." W.K. Kellogg Foundation Press Release 2/17/06.
  http://fconline.fdncenter.org/pnd/10001035/story
  **************** ADVERTISEMENT *********************
Nonprofit Accountability: Are You Doing Enough?
Accountability in the nonprofit world means always being open and ready to answer to those who have invested their trust, faith, and money in your organization. In general, organizations that are accountable can:
    * Raise more money by building public confidence
    * Make processes more effective and jobs easier
    * Spend more time focusing on delivering the mission
Take this 25 question Nonprofit Accountability Assessment to identify areas within your organization to improve accountability and help ensure your organization's long-term health and well-being.
  http://fconline.fdncenter.org/pnd/10001032/blackbaud
  -------------------------<<>>------------------------
(5) Mott Foundation to Support Automotive Industry (2/17/06)

The Charles Stewart Mott Foundation (http://mott.org/) in Flint, Michigan, has awarded two grants totaling $1.2 million to address long- and short-term problems within the domestic automotive industry and their con-sequences for the state's economy.

In an effort to improve the long-term global competitiveness of Michigan's automotive industry, the Center for Automotive Research in Ann Arbor will receive $900,000 for its Program for Automotive Renaissance, which creates new business models designed to make U.S. auto makers more competitive in the global economy and increase their level of cooperation and collaboration with each other. Through PAR, the center will focus on launching and managing up to nine self-sustaining collaborative programs, including the Global Automotive Marketing Alliance, which will assist Michigan supplier groups in marketing their products in North America and overseas, and the Program for Automotive Labor Education, which will address training and certifi- cation needs, focusing initially on students in Bay, Saginaw, and Genesee counties.

(additional stories deleted for space)

::::::::::::::::: PND ON THE WEB :::::::::::::::::

* Classifieds
    http://fdncenter.org/pnd/classifieds/

* Conference Calendar
    http://fdncenter.org/pnd/calendar/

White Hat Communications | 175

FUNDRAISING ONLINE

* Connections
  http://fdncenter.org/pnd/connections/
  http://fdncenter.org/pnd/connections/conn_arch.jhtml

* Job Corner
  http://fdncenter.org/pnd/jobs/

* Message Boards
  http://members4.boardhost.com/PNDtalk/
  http://members5.boardhost.com/ARTStalk/
* Newsmakers
  http://fdncenter.org/pnd/newsmakers/
  http://fdncenter.org/pnd/newsmakers/nwsmkr_arch.jhtml

* NPO Spotlight
  http://fdncenter.org/pnd/spotlight/
  http://fdncenter.org/pnd/spotlight/arch.jhtml

* Off the Shelf
  http://fdncenter.org/pnd/offtheshelf/
  http://fdncenter.org/pnd/offtheshelf/ots_arch.jhtml

* On the Web
  http://fdncenter.org/pnd/ontheweb/
  http://fdncenter.org/pnd/ontheweb/otw_arch.jhtml

* Opinion & Commentary
  http://fdncenter.org/pnd/opinion/index.jhtml

* RFP Bulletin
  http://fdncenter.org/pnd/rfp/

::::::::::: ADVERTISING INFORMATION :::::::::::

PND-L is mailed every Tuesday to more than 65,000 subscribers. For information about ad rates and availability, contact Mitch Nauffts at:
212-807-2433 | mfn@fdncenter.org

::::::::::: FOUNDATION CENTER ONLINE :::::::::::

Have a question about foundations, philanthropy, or fundraising? Visit our online reference service at:

  http://fdncenter.org/learn/librarian/
::::::::::: SUBSCRIBE/UNSUBSCRIBE :::::::::::
To leave this list at any time, send a message to LISTSERV@LISTS.FDNCENTER.ORG with the words
  SIGNOFF PND-L
in the body of your message, or visit our subscription management page at:
  http://fdncenter.org/newsletters/
To rejoin the list at any time, send a message to
LISTSERV@LISTS.FDNCENTER.ORG with the words
  SUBSCRIBE PND-L your name
in the body of the message, or visit us on the Web at:
  http://fdncenter.org/newsletters/
If you have a question or would like more information about the list, send an e-mail to the list administrator at:
MFN@LISTS.FDNCENTER.ORG

Appendix D: Web Writing Issues

For nonprofit organizations, publishing documents on the Web is an effective strategy for reducing the costs of printing, postage, and processing requests for publications. But saving money is only one advantage. Publications can be updated easily and posted, which means that you no longer have to order, or throw out, so many brochures, reports, and other publications when they inevitably become out of date. When your publication is available in camera-ready format, you no longer have to wait days or weeks for it to be sent to a printer and come back printed and bound. It can appear on your Web site within minutes.

It is often a difficult decision to determine who should receive a conventionally printed report, and distribution is often limited because of cost considerations. Publishing the material on the Web permits everyone in the world with Web access (either from their own computer, their work computer, or institutions such as libraries and schools that provide Web access) to read your document. And even if you send me a copy of your organization's annual report in the mail, I may throw it out but then find that I need some information from it. Having it available on your Web site means I can access it immediately, even if I didn't throw out the report, but it is hidden in a stack of papers.

Many organizations have a "restricted access" feature for members, or their board, that denies access to the general public. Sensitive documents can be posted here for a pre-selected audience.

One additional, often overlooked, benefit of publishing material on a Web site is the feature of interactivity. Unlike conventional publishing, publishing on a Web site provides easy opportunities to obtain instant feedback from readers, either by clicking on a "mailto" link, or by filling out an electronic survey form.

To promote visits to your organization's Web site, you need to have content that is attractive to potential visitors. For most nonprofit organizations, that content is specific information that visitors will find useful and cannot obtain anywhere else.

But simply putting your newsletter word-for-word on your Web site, unedited for the Web, is a mistake.

Imagine how you might contrast two scenarios about someone reading your monthly newsletter. The first involves the person reading the version that you send in the mail, and the second is the version you post on your Web site. In the first scenario, the reader is likely to be holding the newsletter, sitting or reclining in a comfortable position in a well-lighted area, starting from the first word, and reading every word (or close to it). In the second scenario, the reader is sitting on a chair, poised in front of a flickering, low-resolution computer monitor, and skimming the content. How do we know the reader is skimming? Research by Jacob Nielsen and John Morkes (see *http://www.useit.com/alertbox/9703b.html*) demonstrates that reading on a computer screen is about 25% slower than reading conventionally, and as a result, only about 16% of Web page viewers read what is on the screen word-for-word.

This argues for a Web writing style that is different from that for "dead tree" publications. First, the articles need to be shorter, preferably in bite-sized morsels that can be seen in one screen. The text is written to facilitate scanning, such as having keywords in bold, and bulleted key points. Headings and subheadings are prominent; there is usually a single idea per paragraph, with space separating these ideas. Pull quotes (short excerpts from the text) may appear in sidebars with larger, more decorative fonts. Most important, ideas are expressed simply in short sentences, and article length overall is typically half of what would be appropriate for conventional publishing.

One convenient feature we have found on some Web pages with very short paragraphs of text and fancy graphics to illustrate them, linked in series, is the availability of a link to large articles unencumbered by graphics, labeled "printer-friendly version." The viewer reads from the series, but prints from the link without the graphics.

Here are ten writing tips for improving your Web pages:

1. Make all content compatible for scanning by the reader. Use bulleted lists and make key words bold.

2. Shorten content to 50% or less of what would appear in a printed publication.

3. Tailor content to needs of your Web audience. The language should be at the level of your audience. Technical requirements, such as using frames, search engines, and file format (e.g. HTML or PDF files) should be at the level of your audience.

4. Take advantage of the Web's interactivity. Seek feedback from the audience by using surveys and "mailto" links to find out what features need to be improved, and what the audience particularly wants to see on your site.

5. Write in a conversational style. In contrast to traditional writing, sentence fragments are acceptable on Web pages. Colloquialisms are also considered

acceptable, assuming the image you want to project is informal. Avoid the passive tense!

6. Limit paragraphs to a single idea/concept. Remember, most readers are skimming and looking for a key concept.

7. Keep sentences short. Any sentence over 20 words is likely to confuse.

8. Correct spelling is still important.

9. Make information your first priority, entertainment second. For almost all nonprofit Web sites, your organization is unlikely to be able to compete with commercial sites that draw their viewers with entertainment. More likely, your viewers will visit your site because they want to know something about an issue on which your organization has expertise and credibility. Capitalize on this by giving the viewer what he/she wants. Flashy animations, jaw-dropping graphics, and slick cartoons are fine, but should be secondary on most nonprofit organizational sites.

10. Label buttons and links so your audience gets what it expects. Creating descriptions of labels, buttons, and links is a form of writing. Think of these as analogous to the newspaper headline—short and descriptive, and a clear, unambiguous summary of the content it seeks to describe.

This Appendix first appeared in Gary Grobman's 2001 book, *The Nonprofit Organization's Guide to E-Commerce*.

Site Review Index

University of Wisconsin-Madison Grants Information Center—Databases (*http:// grants.library.wisc.edu/organizations/computers.html*), 81
VeriSign Internet Trust Services (*http://www.verisign.com*), 152
Web Content Accessibility Guidelines Working Group (*http://www.w3.org/WAI/GL/*), 110
Web Page Backward Compatibility Viewer (*http://www.delorie.com/web/wpbcv.html*), 110
Web Ring, Inc. (*http://dir.webring.com/rw*), 110
Webmonkey (*http://www.webmonkey.com*), 152
WebSurveyor (*http://www.websurveyor.com*), 98
Yahoo! (*http://www.Yahoo.com*),58
Yale Alumni (http://www.aya.yale.edu/), 133
Your Mailing List Provider (*http://www.ymlp.com*), 71
Zoomerang (*http://www.zoomerang.com/web/signup/Basic.aspx*), 98

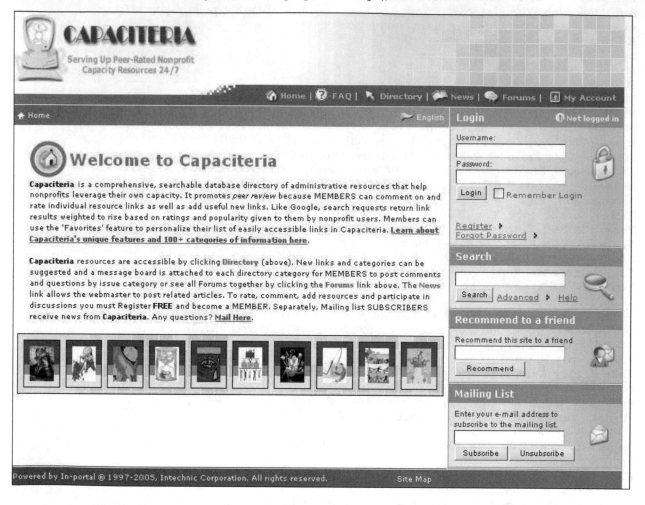

The Capaciteria home page at: http://www.capaciteria.com. Reprinted
with permission. See a review of this Web site on page 116.

Keyword Index

For Further Reading...

There are many helpful books on the market for those interested in finding out more information about online fundraising. We have compiled a list of some of the more recent, valuable publications that are easily accessible from online booksellers, such as Amazon.com and BarnesandNoble.com. The date referred to is the publication date.

Fundraising Basics: A Complete Guide, 2nd Edition by Barbara L. Ciconte
   Publisher: Jones and Bartlett Publishers (2004)

Fundraising For Dummies, 2nd Edition by John Mutz and Katherine Murray
   Publisher: For Dummies (2005)

Fundraising on eBay by Greg Holden and Jill K. Finlayson
   Publisher: McGraw-Hill Osborne Media (2005)

Fundraising on the Internet: The ePhilanthropyFoundation.org's Guide to Success Online, 2nd Edition by Mal Warwick, Ted Hart, Nick Allen (Editors)
   Publisher: Jossey-Bass (2001)

Hank Rosso's Achieving Excellence in Fund Raising (Jossey Bass Nonprofit & Public Management Series) by Eugene R. Tempel (Editor)
   Publisher: Jossey-Bass (2003)

How to Make Money Online with eBay, Yahoo!, and Google by Peter Kent and Jill K. Finlayson
   Publisher: McGraw-Hill Osborne Media (2005)

Introduction to E-Commerce, 2nd Edition by Jeffrey F. Rayport and Bernard J. Jaworski
   Publisher: McGraw-Hill College (2003)

Nonprofit Internet Strategies: Best Practices for Marketing, Communications, and Fundraising Success by Ted Hart, James M. Greenfield, and Michael Johnston
   Publisher: John Wiley & Sons (2005)

Successful Fundraising: A Complete Handbook for Volunteers and Professionals (Second Edition) by Joan Flanagan
   Publisher: McGraw-Hill (1999)

Wired for Good: Strategic Technology Planning for Nonprofits by Joni Podolsky
   Publisher: Jossey-Bass (2003)

About the Authors...

Gary M. Grobman (B.S., Drexel University; M.P.A., Harvard University, Kennedy School of Government; Ph.D., Penn State University) is special projects director for White Hat Communications, a Harrisburg-based publishing and nonprofit consulting organization formed in 1993. He is currently an adjunct professor of Nonprofit Management at Gratz College, where he has taught fundraising and general nonprofit management at the graduate level. He served as the executive director of the Pennsylvania Jewish Coalition from 1983-1996. Prior to that, he was a senior legislative assistant in Washington for two members of Congress, a news reporter, and a political humor columnist for *Roll Call*. He also served as a lobbyist for public transit agencies. In 1987, he founded the Non-Profit Advocacy Network (NPAN), which consists of more than 50 statewide associations that represent Pennsylvania charities. He currently is the Harrisburg Contributing Editor for *Pennsylvania Nonprofit Report*, and is the nonprofit technology/Internet columnist for *Contributions Magazine.* He currently serves on the board of directors of the Greater Harrisburg Concert Band. He also served on the board of directors of the Citizen Service Project, and was the Treasurer of that statewide 501(c)(3), which was established to promote citizen service in Pennsylvania. He is the author of *The Holocaust—A Guide for Pennsylvania Teachers, The Nonprofit Handbook, The Non-Profit Internet Handbook* (co-authored with Gary Grant), *Improving Quality and Performance in Your Non-Profit Organization, The Nonprofit Organization's Guide to E-Commerce*, and other books published by White Hat Communications and Wilder Publications (now Fieldstone). His full biography appears in the current edition of Marquis *Who's Who in America.*

Gary B. Grant received his B.A. in history from the University of Chicago in 1987 and his J.D. from Illinois Institute of Technology, Chicago—Kent College of Law in 1994. In law school, he served on the Chicago Kent Law Review and the Kent Justice Foundation. He worked in the legal clinic providing legal advice to indigent civil defendants and served as an Everett Fellow with Citizens for Tax Justice in Washington, D.C. Gary has spent most of his fundraising career at the University of Chicago. He served as Associate Dean for External Affairs for the School of Social Service Administration and was a Senior Major Gifts officer for the University of Chicago Medical Center. Gary currently serves as the Director of Major Gifts for the National Alzheimer's Association. He is a member of the Association of Fundraising Professionals. Gary lives in Washington, D.C.

Online Fundraising
Reader Survey/Order Form

Return Survey To:
White Hat Communications
PO Box 5390
Harrisburg, PA 17110-0390

My name and address (please print legibly):

1. I would like to suggest the following corrections:

2. I would like to suggest the following topics for inclusion in a future edition:

3. I have the following comments, suggestions, or criticisms:

4. I would like to order _____ additional copies @$29.95 each plus $6 shipping and handling first book, $1 each additional book. Pennsylvania purchasers please add 6% sales tax or include a copy of exemption certificate from the Pennsylvania Department of Revenue. Note: Quantity discounts are available.

The Nonprofit Handbook, 4th Edition
by Gary M. Grobman

The Nonprofit Handbook, Fourth Edition is the most up-to-date and useful publication for those starting a nonprofit or for those already operating one. This 468-page, 35-chapter *Handbook* is based on *The Pennsylvania Nonprofit Handbook*, a book originally published in 1992 with the help of more than two-dozen nonprofit executives and attorneys and now in its 7th edition. Each easy-to-read chapter includes a synopsis, useful tips, and resources to obtain more information. Pre-addressed postcards are included to obtain important government forms, instruction booklets, and informational publications. This essential reference tool includes:

- Information about current laws, court decisions, and regulations that apply to nonprofits—two full pages devoted to each state and the District of Columbia
- Practical advice on running a nonprofit, including chapters on grant-writing, communications, fundraising, quality management, insurance, lobbying, personnel, fiscal management, nonprofit ethics, and 26 other chapters
- Information on applying for federal and state tax-exempt status
- How to write effective grant applications
- How to hire and fire
- Internet resources for nonprofits
- How to develop a strategic plan
- A Guide for students that includes information about the scope, history, theory, and future of the nonprofit sector.

We know you will find *The Nonprofit Handbook* to be an essential resource.
ISBN: 1-929109-13-X   8½" x 11" softcover
468 pages including index
$29.95 U.S. $41.95 Canada

Table of Contents

Foreword by Joe Geiger, Executive Director
PA Association of Nonprofit Organizations

Introduction

Part I For Practitioners

Part II   Student Guide to Nonprofits

"*The Nonprofit Handbook* is must reading. While it will have value as a reference tool to be consulted when needed, I highly recommend that you read the book cover-to-cover to familiarize yourself with the panoply of issues that face the modern nonprofit in the United States."

Joe Geiger, Executive Director
Pennsylvania Association of Nonprofit Organizations

Telephone orders
(Credit card orders):
717-238-3787
Fax orders: 717-238-2090

Online Orders:
http://www.whitehatcommunications.com

PLEASE SHIP MY ORDER TO:

NAME _____

ADDRESS _____

ADDRESS_ _____

CITY/STATE/ZIP _____

TELEPHONE NUMBER _____

❑ Enclosed is a check for $_____ made payable to "White Hat Communications."

❑ Please charge my credit card (VISA, MasterCard, AmEX, or Discover)

Card # _____

Expiration Date _____

3- or 4-digit code (back of card for VISA/MC/DISC; front of card for AMEX) _____

Name as it appears on card _____

Signature _____

Billing address for credit card (if different from above) _____

Billing City/State/Zip _____

Please send the following publications:

QUANTITY	TITLE	AMOUNT
_____	FUNDRAISING ONLINE @ $29.95 each	$ _____
_____	THE NONPROFIT HANDBOOK, 4th EDITION @ $29.95 each	$ _____
_____	OTHER_____	$ _____

Shipping charges: $6.00 first book/$1.00 each additional book in U.S.
Please contact us for rates on rush orders, other methods of shipping, or shipping outside the U.S.

SHIPPING $_____

SUBTOTAL $_____

PA SALES TAX $_____
(6% of subtotal, if applicable)

TOTAL DUE $ _____

Send order form and payment to:
WHITE HAT COMMUNICATIONS
P.O. Box 5390-Dept. 8A
Harrisburg, PA 17110-0390

Federal EIN: 25-1719745

Related Titles Published by White Hat Communications

The Nonprofit Handbook: Everything You Need To Know to Start and Run Your Nonprofit Organization
4th Edition (2005)

The Pennsylvania Nonprofit Handbook
7th Edition (2005)

Days in the Lives of Social Workers
Third Edition (2005)

More Days in the Lives of Social Workers
(2005)

The Social Work Graduate School Applicant's Handbook
Second Edition (2005)

Introduction to the Nonprofit Sector: A Practical Approach for the 21st Century (2004)

The Field Placement Survival Guide (2002)

The Nonprofit Organization's Guide to E-Commerce (2001)

Improving Quality and Performance in Your Non-Profit Organization: An Introduction to Change Management Strategies for the 21st Century (1999)